Breakfast with God is … brilliant!

ROB PARSONS, EXECUTIVE DIRECT

This is fresh, sizzling stuff – don't miss it.

JEFF LUCAS, VICE PRESIDENT, EV

Gerard Kelly is an unexpected kind of person, and *Breakfast with God* is an unexpected approach to meeting the Almighty … he opens up the rich truths of Christian discipleship in an exciting way. I am delighted to commend this book for Christians wrestling to work out how to get time with God each day.

REV RICHARD KEW, EPISCOPAL PRIEST AND WRITER

Filled with sound-bite sized insights, challenges, scripture and prayer, this book will kick-start many into daily spiritual feeding and be an injection of refreshment to the spiritually hungry.

TREV GREGORY, INTERNATIONAL DIRECTOR OF TEMA-MISSION
AND AUTHOR OF *SERIOUS PRAYER*

God used these thoughts to show me more of Jesus and more of myself. Short, to the point and profound – just what I needed to read.

DAVID WESTLAKE, YOUTH DIRECTOR, TEARFUND

They reckon there are two types of people, those who say 'Morning God,' and those who say 'God, it's morning'. *Breakfast with God* is for both types. Whether you are after orange juice, a big breakfast, a continental option or just a strong coffee, *Breakfast with God* nourishes a biblical spirituality for those standing in the foyer of the new millennium.

With his usual gift for words, Gerard Kelly moves easily between the Bible and prayer. *Breakfast with God* is well worth surfing. Or was that serving?

STEVE TAYLOR, POSTMODERN CHURCH PLANTER, GRACEWAY
BAPTIST CHURCH, NEW ZEALAND

Also available from Zondervan

Breakfast with God Volume 1 Duncan Banks
Breakfast with God Volume 3 Roz Stirling
Breakfast with God Volume 4 Simon Hall

Breakfast with God

Volume 2

Gerard Kelly

GRAND RAPIDS, MICHIGAN 49530 USA

We want to hear from you. Please send your comments about this book
to us in care of the address below. Thank you.

GRAND RAPIDS, MICHIGAN 49530 USA
WWW.ZONDERVAN.COM

ZONDERVAN™

Breakfast with God Volume 2
Copyright © 2000 Gerard Kelly

Requests for information should be addressed to:

Zondervan, *Grand Rapids, Michigan 49530*

First published in Great Britain in 2000 by Marshall Pickering.

This edition published in 2002 by Zondervan.

Gerard Kelly asserts the moral right to be identified as the author of this work.

A catalogue record for this book is available from the British Library.

ISBN 0 551 03259 6

Unless otherwise indicated, scripture quotations are taken from the *Contemporary Eng-
lish Version Bible,* © American Bible Society 1991, 1992, 1995.

Scripture quotations marked (NIV) are taken from the *Holy Bible, New International
Version,* © 1973, 1978, 1984 by International Bible Society. Used by permission of Hod-
der & Stoughton Ltd, a member of the Hodder Headline Plc Group. All rights reserved.
'NIV' is a trademark of International Bible Society. UK trademark number 1448790.

Printed and bound in the United Kingdom

02 03 04 05 06 07 08 /MP/ 10 9 8 7 6 5 4 3

This book is dedicated to
Joseph, Aaron, Anna and Jake.

ACKNOWLEDGEMENTS

Many thanks are due to Chrissie, partner in ministry as in marriage, who recalls me often to the character of God, and reminds me of the workings of faith.

Thanks also to all those in the Cyberpub and other arenas who offered ideas for breakfast menus.

Special thanks to the students and tutors of the 1999/2000 LRM course at Cliff College, for being fun to be with.

Gerard Kelly
January 2000

INTRODUCTION

Where do you have yours? On a Paris hotel balcony, with views of the Eiffel Tower, freshly ground coffee and croissants still warm from the bakery? Halfway up a Swiss mountain, with freshly mixed muesli and milk just minutes from the udder? Or on a crowded tube train, where your elbows are pushed so tightly against your side that you can hardly get the Nutri-Grain bar unwrapped?

There is no limit to the places where you can have breakfast. For some it is a rushed affair, for others a leisurely interlude before the business of the day. Some take the healthy option – all fruit and bran and rippling muscles. Others pig out on cholesterol overload.

Whatever your habit, there is one choice that matters more than what you have for breakfast and where you have it – and that's who you have it with. The purpose of this book is to encourage you to have breakfast with God – to carve out, at the beginning of the day, spiritual space in a material world.

Like a healthy breakfast, these few moments of quiet reflection and prayer can change the way the whole day turns. Whether you have time to linger over a full breakfast, or are drinking coffee from a styrofoam cup in the last three seconds before work begins, you need a conversation with the Creator to set you up for the day ahead.

Choose the place. Make the time. Take the trouble. Let breakfast with God be the daily diet that makes the difference in your life.

Orange Juice
'I am the way and the truth and the life!' Jesus answered. 'Without me, no-one can go to the Father.'

JOHN 14:6

THE POWER OF ONE

The Big Breakfast
If you distil fruit juice, you get alcohol. If you boil down a carcass you get bones. If you reduce a perfume to its essence, you get a single, powerful, concentrated fragrance. What do you get if you take 2,000 years of Christianity and similarly reduce it?

According to Hans Küng – perhaps the most respected theologian alive today – you get Jesus. He writes: 'Christianity does not stand or fall by an impersonal idea, an abstract principle, a universal norm, a purely conceptual system … Christianity stands and falls by a concrete person, who represents a cause, a whole way of life: Jesus of Nazareth.'

No matter how religious those who follow Christ become, no matter how complex their systems of theology, the heart of the matter remains a tangible person. It is this that has made the Christian faith so durable, so adaptable, so attractive over 2,000 years of exploration and diversity. And it is with this that the 21st Century must do business – not the system of *Christianity* but the person of *Christ*.

Continental
How much of your spiritual investment is in the system of Christianity, and how much is in the person of Christ?

Coffee
To you we come, O Lord, the true goal of all human desiring. Beyond all earthly beauty, gentle protector, strong deliverer; from first light be our joy.
(From *Celebrating Common Prayer*, London, Mowbray, 1994)

Orange Juice
The Word was in the world, but no one knew him.

JOHN 1:10

BLIND DATE

The Big Breakfast
Austin Powers, International Man of Mystery, is among other things a master of disguise. Like other super-agents before him, he must know how to insinuate himself into a new and foreign situation without being detected.

This is not true of that other man of mystery, Jesus. God's 'disguise' was not deliberately chosen to deceive us. The reverse is true – the incarnation is an act of self-exposure: it makes God more visible, not less.

But the idea of God becoming a human being is so audacious, so strange to our eyes, that when he comes we don't see him! So perfect is God's act of taking on humanity, so complete is his adoption of our nature, that we fail to recognize him. Even in a police line-up, we could so easily pass over Jesus as just another human. Only when God opens our eyes do we begin to see who Jesus really is.

With a number of significant exceptions, those who witnessed the life of Christ did not see him as God. But those who did were so changed by what they saw that they went on to change the world.

Continental
Like a *Blind Date* winner, Jesus waits behind the screen of our perceptions. Only when the screen is rolled back do we begin to see the truth.

Coffee
I open my eyes, Lord, to see you. I open my heart to receive you. I open my life to be your dwelling-place.

Orange Juice

He came into his own world, but his own nation did not welcome him.

JOHN 1:11

HOME SWITCHED HOME

The Big Breakfast

You've had a long and tiring journey. You are jet-lagged, but glad to be home. You park in your own drive, walk to your own front door and put your own key in the lock.

But the lock doesn't turn. You try other keys, but nothing fits. When you see movement in the house, you knock on the door. A total stranger comes and informs you that the house is no longer your home. It has been occupied by the Revolutionary Army of Something-or-Other and has been declared a Stateless Zone. The locks have been changed and you will not be given access. Until you can get a Court Order and police back-up, you are homeless.

This is your home – your property. Not only do you own the title deeds – you even built the place with your own hands. Inside are your belongings, your memories. But you are outside – left out in the cold.

Jesus came to a planet over which he has rights of ownership and occupation – he came to his home. It is we, the tenants, who have refused to give him access.

Continental

Imagine Michael Jordan being refused entry to a Chicago Bulls game. Imagine Bill Gates being thrown out of Microsoft HQ as a trespasser. Now picture God, unrecognized within his own creation.

Coffee

Take your place, Lord Jesus, in my heart and home. May you find warmth and welcome, and sustenance and rest.

Orange Juice

Yet some people accepted him and put their faith in him. So he gave them the right to be the children of God.

JOHN 1:12

ARE YOU RECEIVING ME?

The Big Breakfast

The doors are locked and bolted, the windows barred. A repossession order in hand, the landlord stands at the threshold. The papers prove that he is the rightful owner – the law is on his side and his ultimate victory is assured.

But there is a standoff. His determination to gain entry is matched, ounce for ounce, by the determination of those within to resist.

So he changes tack. Rather than force entry, he announces to all those who will recognize his right of ownership and make themselves known, that a place will be kept for them in the house once repossession is complete. They have one last chance to join the winning side.

But to do so will mean breaking ranks with the rebels. It will mean acknowledging the illegitimacy of the occupation and identifying with the lone figure at the door. It is a hard choice to make – especially from within the occupied home. But the promise is there – a full pardon, and the right to live now the life that is promised for the cosmos.

Continental

Making the choice, identifying with Christ, means breaking ranks with those with whom we have shared the occupation. It is a new allegiance that will often run counter to allegiances we have held in the past.

Coffee

Jesus, who stands at the door of our lives, we welcome you. Jesus, who knocks, and will not come in without invitation, we receive you. Jesus, who promises a new kind of life here and now, we worship you.

Orange Juice

They were not God's children by nature…God himself was the one who made them his children.

JOHN 1:13

WOMB WITH A VIEW

The Big Breakfast

Where you are born, how you are born, to *whom* you are born – these factors affect our lives very deeply.

To be born on the wrong side of the tracks; to be born into wealth and title; to be born and unwanted – we each carry both the burdens and the blessings of our birth. We are not predetermined by our birth like automatons, but we are profoundly shaped by its circumstances.

Right at the start of his Gospel of new birth, John wants us to know that the rebirthing he is talking about is a different quality of birth. There is the possibility of a new start, a new injection of DNA, a whole new inheritance to come into. In our first birth, the choices, characters and circumstances of our parents shape us. In the new birth, we become heirs of God. For John, the encounter with Christ is not just a fork in the road of life; it is an entirely new road to walk.

Continental

John is saying, 'Whatever else you do or don't understand about Christ, understand *this*: the choice to follow Christ is a choice to begin a new kind of life.'

Coffee

Thank you, Father, for the DNA of Jesus. Thank you for the new birth that leads to a new kind of life. Thank you for giving me the right to become your child.

Orange Juice

The Word became a human being and lived here with us. We saw his true glory, the glory of the only Son of the Father.

JOHN 1:14

WAIT UNTIL YOU SEE THE WHITES OF HIS EYES

The Big Breakfast

Meanwhile, back at the squat, nothing has happened to break the stalemate. The offer is there for the rebels to join the landlord now, and be guaranteed a place in his future plans.

But he is not convinced that many will make that choice from a distance. There is only one thing for it. Piercing his eyebrows, nose and ears, the landlord dies his hair orange, puts on his shredded jeans, buys a pet rat and … moves into the squat, becomes one of us, gets close enough for us to see the whites of his eyes. And when we do, we see in them the glory of the Father.

Glory is what Jesus gave up to become human – but you can't rub out something so radiant. When he came to live in our squat, the glory was still visible. We have seen it.

Eve and Adam, the woman and the man, were made in God's image. Jesus finds that image in the human condition and polishes it, until it shines out from his eyes.

Continental

At one time, the glory of God was so distant and powerful that to look upon it would bring death. Even Moses had to turn his face from God. But here is that same God, wrapping himself in flesh, and inviting us to look upon him.

Coffee

Thank you, Lord God, for wrapping your glory in flesh. Thank you for making heaven accessible. Thank you for moving into my neighbourhood.

Orange Juice

John spoke about him and shouted, 'This is the one I told you would come! He is greater than I am, because he was alive before I was born.'

JOHN 1:15

A HOME IN HISTORY

The Big Breakfast

There are two sides to the miracle of the incarnation. The first is the divinity of the equation – it was God himself who came. The second is its sheer physicality – it was to our ordinary world that he came.

John has dealt with the glory – now here's the grit. John the Baptist gets a mention not only for his role in God's plan of salvation, but also because reference to him locates Jesus very precisely in space and time. The Word did not become flesh in some idealized, existential or disembodied sense: the Word became flesh in a specific place and time. Jesus did not 'become human', he became *a* human. John the Baptist is a known figure; his name pinpoints Jesus very specifically in history.

John the Gospel-writer wants to be sure to give to Jesus a place in the flow of time – there was a time before he came, there is a time when he comes and there will be a time beyond his coming. This is history, not just theology.

Continental

For the Christian, theology (i.e. thinking about God) is rooted in history (i.e. knowing what God has done).

Coffee

Into the real world, the flesh-and-blood world, *he came*. Into real family, living in real society, *he came*. Into real, time-and-date-delineated history, *the eternal Son of God came*.

Orange Juice

From the fullness of his grace we have all received one blessing after another.

JOHN 1:16 NIV

SHAKIN' THE TREE

The Big Breakfast

Shake an apple tree in winter, and what do you get? A lone leaf might float to the ground or a broken twig might break loose. Or maybe nothing. Shake a barren tree, and the result is much the same.

But shake a fruitful tree at harvest time, when the apples are ripe and ready, and you will have a different experience. Apples falling on your head. Apples rolling across the grass. Apples piling up at your feet. Newton might never have explained gravity if he had not picked the right tree in the right season. It is from fullness that fruit falls – where there has been growth, where each fruit has ripened until it is almost too heavy for the branch that holds it.

So it is, John tells us, with grace. Jesus came into the world so full of grace, so heavy with fruit, that all who know him are blessed. Not just one blessing, nor the occasional blessing, but one blessing after another, a torrent of blessings tumbling down like ripe apples on our heads. When you shake the tree of Jesus, blessings fall.

Continental

With the coming of Jesus, the tide has turned. The walls of our sand-castle lives are breached – and in flows grace.

Coffee

Where there is barrenness, where we are tired and dry, *let grace fall*. Where there is anger, where bitterness is the only fruit of our lives, *let grace fall*.

Orange Juice

For the law was given through Moses; grace and truth came through Jesus Christ.

JOHN 1:17 NIV

THE LAST PIECE OF THE PUZZLE

The Big Breakfast

There are few figures in the history of Israel who loom larger than Moses – founder of the nation; giver of the Law; leader of the people through the most significant 40 years of their history. Of all the Hebrew giants, Moses is the tallest.

In Christian history, too, he plays a huge part. The Jewish/Christian co-operation over the filming of Steven Spielberg's *Prince of Egypt* bears witness to this shared regard for this shepherd, politician, theologian and military leader.

Moses is important in God's plan of salvation. But he is not the whole picture. Stop with Moses, John tells his Jewish audience, and you have half a story. You have a puzzle with the final, crucial pieces missing. You have an unfinished symphony. You have a lottery ticket with only four numbers chosen. You have a quiz that asks the questions, but goes off air before the answers can be given.

It is Jesus who completes the picture. Jesus brings grace and truth – the last two pieces without which the puzzle makes no sense. Jesus is the completion of Israel.

Continental

If the Law of Moses told us how we should behave, it is the grace and truth of Jesus that enable us to do so.

Coffee

May Jesus who brings completeness to an ancient Law bring the same completeness to my faith. May the Christ who brings fulfilment to the words and works of Moses bring that same fulfilment to my life.

Orange Juice
No-one has ever seen God, but God the One and Only, who is at the Father's side, has made him known.

JOHN 1:18 NIV

GUESS WHO!

The Big Breakfast
There are several things that God is not ashamed to admit – and one of them is that he is invisible from the vantage-point of planet earth. Nowhere in the dealings of the Creator with his creatures does he lay claim to easy visibility. The creature–Creator relationship is dogged by a restricted field of vision.

But John wants us to know that in Jesus this invisible God has chosen to make himself known. And he does so quietly, with little by way of cosmic fanfare. There is no universal announcement, no loud and unmissable disembodied voice. Just the barely audible whisper of a baby born in obscurity. Not only does God squeeze the fullness of his being into the tiniest of forms, but he does so without waking the neighbours.

It is as though, at the very moment when we are searching the horizon, waiting for God's big entrance, he sneaks up behind us, holds his hands to our eyes and says 'Guess Who!'

Continental
God so rarely comes to us in the ways we are looking for. We watch the front door, but he calls at the back door; we expect him in laughter, but he arrives in tears; we seek him in a crowd, but he meets us alone.

Coffee
God of surprises, Father of fun, help me today to find you in the unexpected places where you hide.

Orange Juice
One day, Moses was taking care of the sheep and goats of his father-in-law, Jethro, the priest of Midian.

EXODUS 3:1

FALLING INTO FAILURE

The Big Breakfast
If you're going to fail, fail in style. Moses had tried to act on behalf of his birth-tribe, defending a slave against one of his own adopted people, the Egyptians. But it all went pear-shaped, and he found himself in exile, living in the rocky, infertile hills of Midian, scratching an income tending sheep – a job beneath contempt for an Egyptian.

Brought up in the palaces of Pharaoh, in the abundant fertility of the Nile River valley, Moses was trained to reign. As a non-Egyptian, he would never be the Pharaoh himself – but the film *Prince of Egypt* is right in showing that he was destined to be the ruler's close confidant.

From celebrity to slavery, from royalty to rejection, Moses had fallen as far as it is possible to fall and still be conscious. But God had never given up on this impetuous ruler. Late in life, just as the slow decline was beginning, the Redeemer stepped in.

Past mistakes need not rob us of God's future. It ain't over 'til the fat bush burns.

Continental
What disqualifies you from making something of your life for God? Too old? Too tired? Tried too many times already? Take a look at Moses and think again.

Coffee
Father of failures, God of the good-for-nothing, hope of the has-been – let your redeeming fire touch my life this day.

Orange Juice
But Moses said, 'Who am I …?'

EXODUS 3:11

MIRROR, MIRROR IN THE SKY

The Big Breakfast
Moses' initial curiosity about God's identity is carried in his body language. He moves towards the bush, staring deep into the fire – probably trembling with fear. He doesn't need to speak, as God takes the initiative by introducing himself.

The first question that Moses *does* utter is not Paul's 'Who are you, Lord?' but 'Who am I?' It is his own identity that he struggles with – who is he that God should choose and use him? It is not always our questions about who God is that stop us from serving him, but our questions about who we are.

God's answer to Moses is instructive – 'I will be with you.' Moses' adequacy is to be found in God – God is to be the mirror in which the tired old shepherd sees himself and is renewed.

In an age in which self-identity changes with one's mood and self-reinvention is all the rage – a hall of mirrors in which every turn screams back to us 'Be this way!' – God offers us the sure and stable mirror of his presence in which to find out who we are.

Continental
How might looking deeper into God change the way you see yourself?

Coffee
When confusion saps our confidence and self-questioning clouds our way, help us, Father, to see clearly in the mirror of your presence.

Orange Juice

Moses said to God, 'Suppose I go to the Israelites and say to them, "The God of your fathers has sent me to you," and they ask me, "What is his name?" Then what shall I tell them?'

EXODUS 3:13 NIV

WHOM SHALL I SAY IS CALLING?

The Big Breakfast

This verse is often quoted as evidence for Moses' lack of faith, as if he is using his questions to put off the dreadful moment when he must simply believe God. There is another possibility. These questions may in fact be evidence of the great wisdom of Moses.

Even as he asks, he is demonstrating why it is that God has chosen him above all others. Wisdom tells Moses that it is all very well *him* meeting God in a bush – but if those to whom he goes have no grasp on that experience, he will simply appear mad.

With the bush still burning, and the encounter in full swing, Moses is already thinking ahead to the cold light of tomorrow, when he will have no such props to help him. He needs not only to encounter God, but also to be able to explain. He asks God for a spiritual currency that is *transferable*.

How much fuller might our churches be if those of us who seek to encounter God worked as hard at seeking to explain?

Continental

What qualities make our experience of God *transferable*? What makes it easier – or harder – to tell others about the God whom we have encountered?

Coffee

God may meet you in divine confrontation at the Burning Bush – but can you explain it in mundane conversation at the Boring Bus Stop?

Orange Juice

God said to Moses: 'I am the eternal God. So tell them that the LORD, whose name is 'I AM', has sent you.

EXODUS 3:14

WHAT'S IN A NAME?

The Big Breakfast

God's self-declaration as 'I AM' contains, by implication, its own opposite – the 'I AM NOT' of the Creator. If God were to choose a name for himself, he would immediately be seen – by Israelite, Egyptian and Midianite alike – as one god among many. Every hillside, every tribe, every region and nation – in some cases every household – had its own pet god in Moses' day. Some were more powerful than others; some were localized; some came close to overall supremacy – but none ruled unchallenged. To be a god was to join a hall of fame as full as any Hollywood roll call or sports museum of today. By saying 'I AM' (from which the Hebrew name *Yahweh*, 'HE IS', was derived) God was setting himself above and beyond the crowd. 'I AM NOT' local; 'I AM NOT' the god of one tribe alone; 'I AM NOT' tied to time or place. In these two words, 'I AM', Moses has been introduced to the Creator of the cosmos – the in-all, above-all, once-for-all God.

Continental

No wonder the Jewish leaders were so shocked, generations later, when Jesus used the words 'I AM' of himself.

Coffee

Father, forgive us for making you small and local – open our eyes to your cosmos-spanning glory!

Orange Juice
The LORD answered, 'What's that in your hand?'

EXODUS 4:2

BRING AND BUY!

The Big Breakfast

Moses is beginning to warm to the possibility of freedom. All the passion he felt when he first rediscovered his Hebrew roots, when he saw the slavery of his people and longed to act, is coming back to him. Decades of forgetting are being peeled away.

But he is not yet sold on God's call. He wonders what weapons he will have if his first approach is rebuffed. With sharp insight, he foresees the stubbornness of the Hebrews – and asks God what Phase 2 of the plan might be. God's answer is the timeless, universal, unchanging question that he puts to each of us: 'What do you have in your hand?'

We seek God for *his* gifts – he seeks ways to use *ours*. We ask him, 'What can you give us?' He asks us, 'What do you bring?' We see faith as a supermarket for buying new gifts – God sees it as a bring-and-buy sale where no one arrives empty-handed. Before God overwhelms you with some new gift, he will always ask you, 'What do you have in your hand?'

Continental
Consider the areas of your life in which you are longing for God to act. Ask yourself, 'What do I have in my hand?'

Coffee
Lord God, all that I have in my hands – my talents and my lack of talent, my background and my brokenness, my humanity and my helplessness – I bring to you.

Orange Juice

'A staff,' he replied.

The LORD said, 'Throw it on the ground.'

EXODUS 4:2-3 NIV

A LIFE LESS ORDINARY

The Big Breakfast

The staff that Moses carried was more than a stick. It was symbolic of everything that had kept him out of Egypt – his job as a shepherd; his home on the rocky mountain-side; his escape into an 'ordinary life'; his exile from both the home of his adoption and the tribe of his birth.

Without failure, Moses would have had no staff. Without weakness he would not have needed it. When he threw it on the ground, he threw with it the last 40 years of his life. The power of God came at the point of Moses' weakness – it was his failure that was transformed, not his success. The most ordinary object of Moses' experience was transformed to lead him to a life less ordinary.

From this point on, the staff remained with Moses. Thrown before Pharaoh, it confounded the darkest magicians of the day. Held high over a raging sea, it parted waves. Struck against a rock, it brought water in the desert. But in becoming the symbol of God's power, not once did it cease to be the symbol of Moses' weakness.

Continental

God meets with us not in the place of our strength, but in the place of our weakness. His power finds fruitful ground in our failure.

Coffee

God of transforming power, take the ordinary things of our lives – the unspectacular and the unsuccessful – and equip us for a life less ordinary.

Orange Juice

Jesus declared, 'I tell you the truth, no-one can see the kingdom of God unless he is born again.'

'How can a man be born when he is old?' Nicodemus asked. *JOHN 3:3-4 NIV*

INHERIT THE WIND

The Big Breakfast

Nicodemus might well ask. He was not only old; he was also educated, wealthy, powerful, significant, competent and respected. He was everything a religious leader of his generation might want to be – and everything a new-born baby is not. He was so scared of change that he went to see Jesus under cover of darkness.

Jesus issued a direct challenge – he called him to swap his competence for newness, his knowledge for ignorance, his certainties for mysteries and his faith in a static, unchanging God for a living relationship with 'the wind that blows where it wants to'. Jesus asked him to give up religion and inherit the wind.

How many of us in today's religious institutions – who call ourselves 'born again' and are as sure of our faith as Nicodemus was of his, until he met Christ – stand in just as much need of such a change as Nicodemus did?

Continental

The things that have got you to where you are today are not the things that will get you to where you need to be tomorrow.

George Barna

Coffee

Blessed are you, God of compassion and mercy. In the darkness of my life, let your light break forth in new birth.

Orange Juice
But when the time was right, God sent his Son …

GALATIANS 4:4

AN IDEA WHOSE TIME HAS COME

The Big Breakfast
The 'Pregnancy Principle', used in management training, states that it takes one pregnant woman nine months to produce a baby – but nine pregnant women given one month won't do it. Some things just have to take their course. Once they have taken their course (ask any mother), nothing can stop them. There is no power on heaven or earth that will stop a baby being born once the time is right.

For Jesus, Paul is saying, the time was right. Heaven was pregnant with mercy. God was longing for the day – it was the moment that the whole cosmos had been moving towards. When the time came, nothing would be the same again.

Never, until Jesus, had such an audacious idea been proposed. Far from forcing men to seek him, God himself would seek them. The great gulf between God and humankind would be bridged not from the human side but from God's. Once the moment was right, nothing could hold back the flood. The cross was an idea whose time had come.

Continental
The coming of Christ was God's initiative, God's intervention, and God's idea. While religion is so often about women and men seeking God, Jesus embodies the very reverse.

Coffee
Jesus, born of Mary, I welcome your initiative of mercy. You made the choice to seek me out – I make the choice to receive.

Orange Juice

God sent the Spirit of his Son into our hearts, the Spirit who calls out, 'Abba, Father.'

GALATIANS 4:6 NIV

THE FAITH OF THE FATHERLESS

The Big Breakfast

The psychologist Paul Vitz, of New York University, has claimed recently that atheism is 'the faith of the fatherless'. All the key figures in the historic rejection of God, he notes, struggled with absence or abuse in their relationship with their fathers.

While Freudian psychology has claimed for generations that belief in God is a projection of the desire for a father, Vitz clearly shows that the same is true of *unbelief*. Christianity, for Vitz as for the Apostle Paul, is the faith of restored fatherhood.

Not since Eve and Adam walked with God in the cool of the evening has it been possible to know the intimacy captured in the word *Abba* (the Aramaic word for 'father'). This is the ultimate triumph of Christ, not only that rebellion is dealt with, but that relationship is restored. Pulsing in this cry of *Abba* is a longing that has dominated the heart of God since the gates of Eden swung shut. Slavery is over. Christ has made us daughters and sons once again.

Continental

In New Testament times the word *Abba* would not have been used in the case of an adoption until the decision was final, permanent and unequivocal. What would it be like for a child adopted out of slavery to say *Abba* for the first time?

Coffee

Abba-God, you have adopted me from slavery and death to be your child. Thank you for being the parent I have always longed for.

Orange Juice

... since you are a son, God has made you also an heir.

GALATIANS 4:7 NIV

HEIRS AND GRACES

The Big Breakfast

There is a sense in which our adoption looks to the past. It sees the poverty and slavery from which we have been delivered, and rejoices in the God of liberation. In another sense, it is a present experience – enjoying the companionship and security of God, the perfect parent.

But there is a third dimension to our adoption, in that it has a future tense. All that was lost in the fall, all the Creator's ambitions for his human friends, all the cosmic significance of the role to which Eve and Adam were called – all this is restored to us once more, as we are called not children only, but also heirs.

To enter into the parenthood of God is to enter into a destiny beyond our imagining. It is this future dimension of the cross that gives it irresistible power – the power of hope for the hopeless, the power of inheritance for the dispossessed.

Continental

There are promises of God that are fulfilled the moment we come into adoption – the promise of forgiveness is one. But there are other promises – the fullness of healing and restoration – that may remain in the future for us.

Coffee

God of my adoption, Father Son and Spirit, thank you that you have dealt with my past history, you have transformed my present experience, and you have given me a future full of promise.

Orange Juice
You reached down from heaven, and you lifted me from deep in the ocean.

PSALM 18:16

INCARNATION STREET

The Big Breakfast
Ever dropped your car keys down a drain? More often than not, Mercy's Law dictates that they are not washed away, but land on a shelf not far below the drain-cover.

But Murphy's Law follows closely behind, dictating that they are too far away to reach. You can see them glinting in the shadows, but nothing you can do reaches them. A coat-hanger isn't long enough to hook them. Physical contortions aren't enough to get your arm through the grill of the drain-cover. And shouting at them generally achieves nothing.

You have only two options. You can abandon your keys. Or you can prise open the drain-cover and climb down. Only the second option will get your car started.

Even before Christ, the Bible anticipates the notion of God 'reaching down' for us. When nothing else will save us, God himself takes the initiative to reach us. In the verse above the Psalmist gives a trailer for the miracle of incarnation, when God not only lifts the drain-cover, but climbs down the ladder himself.

Continental
There is no place so low that God can't reach us. There is no water so deep that he can't draw us out. There is no current so strong that his grip will fail us.

Coffee
God of rescue and redemption, Christ of salvation and safety: reach out to all those who are lost in deep waters. May the strength of your arm and the miracle of incarnation save them.

Orange Juice
You rescued me from enemies, who were hateful and too powerful for me.

PSALM 18:17

THE FIRST
EMERGENCY SERVICE

The Big Breakfast
There is no one harder to rescue than the person who thinks they are not in trouble. There is no one harder to help than the one who says, 'I can handle it.' Whatever experience the author of this Psalm had been through, he was unafraid to admit his own limitations. The enemies *were* too strong.

How many of us get into difficulty when we underestimate the force of our enemies? Alcohol, drugs, debt, dysfunctional emotions and patterns of behaviour, sexual addictions – these and a thousand other forces can become too strong for us. Like river currents, these things start out in our lives at a strength we can swim against. But momentum builds; the currents grow stronger; we are drawn out of our depth. Before we realize it, we are being carried away.

Without outside help, our situation can only get worse. Rescue, in that moment, turns on our willingness to admit to our need of help. Pride fights against the admission of failure: but that admission may be the first, vital step towards rescue.

Continental
The successful human life is not the life that knows no weakness or failure and needs no help. It is the life that knows when to admit to weakness, when to acknowledge failure, and when to ask for help.

Coffee
God who reaches out to those in need, God who rescues those in trouble, God who gives strength to those whose enemies are strong – reach out to me this day.

Orange Juice

They confronted me in the day of my disaster, but the LORD was my support.

PSALM 18:18 NIV

MORE THAN A BAD-HAIR DAY

The Big Breakfast

When I was mourning the death of my mother, I managed to keep my emotions at bay for several days. I was deeply shocked, but life somehow went on.

A few days after her death, though, I went to get something from the freezer in the garage. I discovered that one of the children had left the freezer door open overnight: it had defrosted, and all the food was ruined. All that was left of its frozenness was a growing puddle on the floor. Somehow, looking at this small-scale disaster, all my inner pain rose to the surface. I collapsed in tears of grief and exhaustion and spent the next 24 hours in bed.

It took a domestic crisis to break my defences, to force me to face up to my grief. Sometimes it takes a day of disaster to get us to deal with our problems. It is not until we are desperate, with our enemies gloating over us, that we cry for help. But that's where God is. Like the most dramatic of movie plot-lines, it is just when all is lost that all is found.

Continental

Don't be surprised that God allows the day of disaster to overtake you. Very often, it is the very thing you need to force a rescue.

Coffee

Thank you, Father, that you are with us when disaster falls. On the worst days, you mount your rescue plans. It is when we are most lost that you are most able to save us.

Orange Juice
He brought me out into a spacious place; he rescued me because he delighted in me.

PSALM 18:19 NIV

WELCOME TO THE WIDE OPEN COUNTRY

The Big Breakfast
Marlboro Country is that fictitious part of America where a screen-wide sky is always blue; where cow-hands with chiselled chins are dressed in Gap clothes; where all is space and freedom, and you can't see the cancer wards or hear the coughing.

The persistence and power of the image is evidence of the survival of an ancient idea, familiar to the Hebrew mind – the idea of salvation as a 'wide open space'. An open landscape spoke to the Hebrews of new opportunities and challenges; of freedom from slavery; of the promise of prosperity and fruitfulness. The same sense of hope and adventure that opened up the American West is present in this abiding image of 'a spacious place'.

Salvation is not just about buying a ticket to heaven – it is about living an eternal kind of life now. It is a life of new possibilities; a life brimming with potential. For those who have made mistakes in the past, it is a fresh beginning. For those who have never known creative freedom, it is a land of opportunity.

Continental
Salvation is not a turnstile that you pass through: it is a landscape that opens up before you.

Coffee
Wide open is the landscape into which my God has brought me. Wide open is my heart to new beginnings.

Orange Juice
Our Father in heaven …

MATTHEW 6:9

THE ULTIMATE OVERVIEW

The Big Breakfast
Why do tennis umpires sit on elevated chairs? Why is the weather best understood through satellite imaging? Why do eagles hunt from such a great altitude? The answer, in every case, is 20-20 high-sight. You get a view of a situation from a great height that you cannot get on the ground.

Prayer, according to Jesus, is rooted not only in *who* God is – the Father who made us and loves us – but also in *where* God is. Heaven is the ultimate vantage point, offering an overview of our needs that is invisible from any other angle.

Those four words cited above – almost certainly the most-quoted words in the Bible – capture the twin reality that is the engine-room of biblical prayer. Because God is in heaven, he is distant from us, far enough away to take an eagle's-eye view of our lives and to lead us well. Because he is our Father, that distance does nothing to dent his commitment to us. Prayer is a message sent over the wire to Headquarters. At the same time it is a word whispered in the ear of a concerned parent.

Continental
'Sometimes you're further than the moon,' writes Martin Smith of the band Delirious, 'sometimes you're closer than my skin.' Both God's distance from us and his closeness to us are necessary for the effectiveness of prayer.

Coffee
Father, I know so little of prayer. Standing with your first disciples in their ignorance and need, I echo their words: 'Lord, teach us to pray.'

Orange Juice
... hallowed be your name ...

MATTHEW 6:9 NIV

CLEANING UP GOD'S IMAGE

The Big Breakfast
Computer-based graphics and imaging
programmes offer a range of 'clean-up' tools,
from image sharpening to de-speckling. My
favourite is a command called 'Remove Noise'. This analyses
the bit-map of an image and looks for random pixels that
don't contribute anything useful and are getting in the way. It
is the digital equivalent of blowing across a chalk drawing to
remove the dust without disturbing the picture.

This process is something like what is at work in the phrase
'Hallowed be thy name'. To ask that the name of God should
be honoured is the same, in Hebrew culture, as asking that his
character should be known and seen. We are praying here
that the clutter and distractions of our lives – the dust and
debris that stops us seeing God for who he is – might be
swept away, until the Father can clearly be seen and known.

Whatever else this important phrase means, it is a 'Remove
Noise' command for our life of prayer.

Continental
A number of people
have experienced
trouble on the
Internet when
hackers have been
able to hijack their
name and use it to
access suspect
websites and even to
make purchases. In
what senses have we
hijacked the name of
God?

Coffee
Father, as we learn to pray and grow in faith, may our prayers – and our actions
– be a true reflection of your character and name.

Orange Juice
... your kingdom come, your will be done ...
MATTHEW 6:10 NIV

HAVE IT YOUR OWN WAY ...

The Big Breakfast
We are all kingdom-carriers. Each of us has a sphere of activity and influence over which we are able to exercise authority. Much of this is inward and unseen, but it spills over into our visible lives. At times our 'kingdom' only matters to us, but there are also times when others are drawn into our sphere.

To ask that God's kingdom come is not to pray for some fundamentalist state in which the whole of life looks like church. Rather, it is to pray that more and more of the visible world will be drawn into the sphere of God's influence and rule – that rebellion will end and obedience to God will break out like springtime.

We want God's will to be done because God has all the best ideas about how things should be. Everything in the creation is designed, at its heart, to respond to the expressed love of its Creator. Things function best when they function in God, where the response of love is heartfelt and unhindered. It is for this condition that we pray.

Continental
As I pray 'Your will be done', I must be willing to change where I am the hindrance, and I must be willing to co-operate in the fulfilling of God's purposes.

Coffee
Father, I want what you want for my life and for the world. And where I find it hard to want what you want, I want to want what you want!

Orange Juice

... on earth as it is in heaven.

MATTHEW 6:10 NIV

MY HOUSE IS YOUR HOUSE

The Big Breakfast

Imagine visiting friends who have bought a new house or apartment and have spent months decorating it.

Not only is it beautifully presented and perfectly maintained, but these friends are also prodigies of household organization. There are systems for washing and washing up, systems for garbage disposal and recycling. Despite having 10 lively children, 16 pets, 3 full-time jobs, 19 hobbies and 43 committee memberships, your friends live a quiet and peaceful life.

Whenever you visit, there is a cake just baked, a fire just lit and a martini just martinied, and a fresh pot of coffee is flooding the house with its aroma. And they have time to sit and talk.

What would you ask of such friends, if you were allowed to ask anything? 'Please come and run my home the way you run yours!' We could say that this is what the above prayer means. We want the place where we live to look like the place where God lives. Whatever it takes, we want our home to be run like his.

Continental

In heaven the will of God is done immediately – without delay or dispute, without procrastination or protest. What might the earth be like if the same were true of us?

Coffee

If in heaven no injustice, no injustice on earth! If in heaven no starvation, no starvation on earth! If in heaven no deceit, no deceit on earth! Whatever cannot stand in heaven, let it be torn down on earth.

Orange Juice
... on earth as it is in heaven.
MATTHEW 6:10 NIV

TRENDS OF THE EARTH

The Big Breakfast
In the teachings of Jesus, in most instances, the name *heaven* is used to denote the source or origin of the will of God. Heaven is where the purposes of God begin; it is the arena of their gestation and development.

The name *earth*, on the other hand, is used to denote the target or destination of God's will. The earth is the arena of God's actions and ambitions. The direction in which the purposes of God flow is not earth to heaven but heaven to earth.

In redemption as in creation, God sees his highest purposes embodied – given substance – in the physical cosmos. Thus to pray 'Your will be done on earth as in heaven' is not to ask for some interim solution – a temporary application of God's will to this world until we all enjoy his presence in the next. It is to co-operate with the highest eternal declaration of God's desire. To think of heaven as a destination is to misunderstand the biblical texts. We are not *going there* to live with God forever – he is *coming here* to live with us.

Continental
The Bible looks forward to a moment of *consummation*, when heaven tumbles out upon the earth and all things are made new.

Coffee
Father, you have promised a day when all things will be brought into obedience to your will; when every knee will bow and all creation will declare your praise. Help me to live, today, in the joyful anticipation of that day.

Orange Juice
Give us our food for today.

MATTHEW 6:11

ENOUGH IS ENOUGH!

The Big Breakfast
There is an ancient Hebrew proverb that offers a valuable expansion of this brief petition. It would have been familiar to Jesus, and was almost certainly in his mind when he taught this prayer.

It reads: 'Don't let me be too poor or too rich. Give me just what I need. If I have too much to eat, I might forget about you; if I don't have enough, I might steal and disgrace your name' (Proverbs 30:8–9).

The author fears two forms of poverty: the grinding, physical poverty that drives women and men into crime and desperation; but equally the spiritual poverty of forgetfulness that comes with wealth. Both are snares that can tear the unwise believer away from God. The petition, 'Please God, don't let me be poor' is counterbalanced by the petition, 'Please God, don't let me be rich.'

In contemporary culture, the first is a prayer we pray daily – with our lifestyles if not our lips. The second is a less familiar cry.

Continental
One of the tasks we accept when we take on the praying of this prayer is the task of finding out just what 'enough' should mean for us. It takes time and effort, but it liberates us to pray with total faith to receive our daily bread.

Coffee
Teach us, Father, to understand the meaning of 'enough'. Forgive us when, through greed, we ask too much of you, and when, through fear, we ask too little.

Orange Juice
Give us today our daily bread.
MATTHEW 6:11 NIV

FAITH IN
THE FILOFAX

The Big Breakfast
A question much loved by time-management gurus is 'How do you eat an elephant?' The answer is 'One steak at a time.' A similar principle operates in this prayer. How do you tackle the huge mountain of needs and challenges that confronts you when you pray? One day at a time.

Elsewhere Jesus has said, 'Each day has enough troubles of its own' (Matthew 6:34 NIV), and while there is an emphasis in this petition on *bread*, there is also an emphasis on it being *daily*. This helps us to pray by giving us focus.

By all means talk to God about all the things that you have to talk to him about. By all means look to the future. But when it comes to asking for specific outcomes and answers – ask yourself, What outcomes do I need today? What is there in your day's schedule that cries out for the intervention of God? Keep tomorrow's troubles under lock and key until the dawn releases them. What do you need *today*?

Continental
Don't let the concerns of tomorrow rob you of the joys of today.

Coffee
Creator God, you made a world that functions in days and nights. You fed your people in the desert on bread for one day only. Help me to understand the rhythm of the days, and to dedicate my prayers – and my action – to the needs of each new day.

Orange Juice
Forgive us our debts, as we also have forgiven our debtors.

MATTHEW 6:12 NIV

THE BIG LET-DOWN

The Big Breakfast
When God forgives us, there is a qualitative as well as a quantitative breadth to his mercy. He forgives us many sins, but he also forgives us many *kinds* of sin.

The sins we find easiest to spot are offences committed against God – direct, identifiable acts of rebellion. To the Hebrew mind, there is much more to sin than this. There is a deeper sense in which sin is a *failure to meet an obligation*. Our debt to God accumulates whenever we fail to meet our obligations to him. In simple terms, we sin whenever we let God down.

This becomes a dynamic definition when we apply it to those in debt to us. We are called to forgive not only those who in some specific way have sinned against us, but all those who have let us down – and even those whom we *feel* have let us down. Whenever we forgive, we are striking a blow against the spirit of the age and for the Spirit of our God.

Continental
The list of those whom we need to forgive grows longer as soon as we extend it to those whose only crime is that they let us down. More names on the list – more opportunities to forgive.

Coffee
Help me, Father, to forgive all those who sin against me, even if they just let me down. And help me to go on forgiving, daily, for as long as it takes.

Orange Juice
And lead us not into temptation …

MATTHEW 6:13 NIV

The Big Breakfast
Harrogate in North Yorkshire is a nice town, by all accounts. I have only been there once, on an occasion when I chose to walk the short distance from the Conference Centre to the station.

It should have taken 10 to 15 minutes, but when 30 had passed, I knew that I was lost. I had a map, of sorts, but this was grade-'A' lostness – the lostness where you can't even see which way up you should be holding the map. When I eventually asked a local and found my way, I discovered that for much of my 40 minutes I had been walking in entirely the wrong direction.

When we are lost, we need help. When we are *really* lost, we need more help than a simple map can give – we need a flesh-and-blood guide who can show us how to read the map, orient us to True North, and set us on our way. The 'Lead us not' of this prayer includes a 'lead us': we will avoid temptations, trials and trouble when we are led by a trustworthy guide.

Continental
God does more than send us a map. He is a guide who walks with us every step of the way. What does it take to hear, and follow, his guidance?

Coffee
Father, I confess that without you I am lost. All the guide-books in the world won't help me when I don't know where to start. Walk with me. Be my guide – and teach me to trust your leading.

Orange Juice

... but deliver us from the evil one.

MATTHEW 6:13 NIV

HOME DELIVERY

The Big Breakfast

The Celtic practice of praying daily for the protection of God over those we know and love has fallen into disuse in more recent centuries. Many of us have lost the sense of danger or conflict. We are distantly aware of opposition to God, but we don't expect it close to home.

But close to home is exactly where we need God's hand. Jesus ends his prayer in no doubt as to the reality, proximity and potency of evil. Whenever you pray, he implies, seek the protection and deliverance of God.

Like taking suntan cream to Majorca, or wearing seat belts on short journeys, seeking the protection of the triune God over every aspect and activity of our lives should be second nature. Prayers for protection over households, over travellers, over places of work – all these and more have their place in the vocabulary of trust. This is not about superstition and fear. It is about a relationship of love and trust with your Father.

Continental

There is nowhere we can go which is beyond God's protection – but it remains an act of trust and love to ask for it.

Coffee

Christ as a light illumine and guide me! Christ as a shield overshadow and cover me! Christ be under me! Christ be over me! Christ be beside me, on left hand and right! Christ be before me, behind me, about me! Christ this day be within and without me!
(St Patrick, quoted in David Adam,
The Wisdom of the Celts, Lion, Oxford, 1996)

Orange Juice
... but deliver us from the evil one.

MATTHEW 6:13 NIV

GLOBAL DELIVERY SYSTEM

The Big Breakfast
This final line of Jesus' prayer answers an unspoken question: When do we stop praying? What is the target toward which we are moving, as we co-operate with God in the coming of his kingdom?

If the 'us' of the Lord's Prayer is not just 'me and mine' but the whole world – if we pray these words as the cry of humanity to its Creator – then the question is answered. We will go on praying, and God will go on listening, until that day when the whole cosmos – every woman, man, child and created thing – is delivered from the evil one. When the deliverance is complete across the planet, we can stop praying, and God, with us, will rest.

But until that day there is no rest. No matter how satiated my own needs might be, while there is need on planet earth, I am called to pray. We ask no less of God than that he will deliver us – all of us – from the very presence of evil.

Continental
The Lord's Prayer is not merely wishful thinking: God has promised us deliverance. There is a day coming when he will wipe away every tear. It is in the certainty of this hope that we pray.

Coffee
A resolution: Understanding that prayer must reach beyond the small concerns of my own needs, and knowing that the cry of humanity reaches to the throne of God, I resolve to pray – and to go on praying – until the day of full deliverance comes.

Orange Juice

As Jesus was leaving the temple, one of his disciples said to him, 'Teacher, look at these beautiful stones and wonderful buildings!'

MARK 13:1

THE TALLEST IDEA IN TOWN

The Big Breakfast

The Sydney Opera House, the World Trade Center in New York, the Millennium Dome … every major city of the world has its stand-out architecture. Big buildings house big ideas – we project our values in bricks and mortar. These projections of ambition and hope become the language of the city – the daily headlines of the urban skyline.

Continental

To read the message of the urban skyline is to hear the heart of the city.

To the disciples, the Temple was simply the most imposing and the most solid building in their lives. Set at the heart of Jerusalem, its huge walls rose above the neighbouring houses to overshadow daily life for all concerned. The message was loud and clear: the traditions of this Temple were immovable at the heart of this community. The biggest ideas in town were ideas associated with the Temple. For the disciples, as for all Jews of their day, this was the uncontested conclusion, and every time they saw the Temple they were reminded.

The message of our day is the same but different. What are the temples of our day? They are threefold: shopping malls and banks, arts and entertainment institutions and, tallest of all, telecom towers.

Coffee

May the glory of your kingdom which the saints enjoy surround our steps as we journey this day.

(Adapted from *Celebrating Common Prayer*, London, Mowbray, 1994)

Orange Juice

... since what may be known about God is plain to them, because God has made it plain to them.

ROMANS 1:19 NIV

I'M OVER HERE!

The Big Breakfast

If you're looking for cold logic, don't watch children playing hide-and-seek. If they're young enough, they will happily stand in the middle of a room, in full view of everyone, and 'hide' by covering their eyes. Logic dictates that to be hidden you must be out of sight, but infant logic knows only one rule – if I can't see you, you can't see me!

Or take the child who has hidden so well that no one comes close to finding her. After a time, the silence of her hiding-place and the excitement of success will get too much. There will be a shuffle and then a cough – and if all else fails she'll start singing. The point of hiding, to a child, is not to avoid being found, but to make being found fun!

Not surprisingly, God is more childish than we are. When he plays hide and seek in the creation, he makes it as easy as possible for us to find him.

Continental

The world resounds with clues to the whereabouts of God. If you're listening hard enough, you will hear him singing.

Coffee

Creator God, thank you that you do not hide from us. You make your presence felt in a million ways each day. Help me, today, to find you in unexpected places.

Orange Juice

For since the creation of the world God's invisible qualities – his eternal power and divine nature – have been clearly seen …

ROMANS 1:20 NIV

PHYSICAL GRAFFITI

The Big Breakfast

Graffiti artists throughout the world are known for their driving desire – their all-consuming passion – to sign their name in every conceivable place.

Spray-can in hand, they will climb unclimbable walls, hang over death-drop bridges and risk all on electrified train tracks – just to make their mark on the world. There is an artistic motivation, but the primary goal is self-identification. A graffiti artist's 'tag' is her or his life. An unsigned work is unthinkable – anonymity defeats the object of the exercise.

For Paul, this same motivation is visible in the works of God. It is not enough to make a good universe – everywhere and in everything, he has signed his work. The word 'since', in this context, also carries the meaning 'from' – it is from the works of God that the character of God spills out. His tag is everywhere – he can be identified by his work. The creation is not only a masterpiece: it is a signed masterpiece.

Continental

The Invisible Man in the classic story of the same name can only be seen by the clothes he wears. Only when bandages are wrapped around his face can the contours of his features be seen. In the same way, God 'clothes' himself in the created world – so that we can see him.

Coffee

To God the Father, who created the world; to God the Son, who redeemed the world; to God the Holy Spirit, who sustains the world; be all praise and glory, now and forever.

Orange Juice

... being understood from what has been made, so that men are without excuse.

ROMANS 1:20 NIV

MORSE CODE

The Big Breakfast

Crosswords are either fascinating or infuriating, depending on your character and preference. But millions of people do them. And millions more will sit for hours watching celebrity sleuths, willing them to get to the end of the mystery, to work the puzzle out.

The mark of a good clue, whether in a crossword or a thriller, is that it takes hard work to solve but, once solved, it is so perfect, so obvious that there can be no doubt. Without the resolution, we feel cheated. But without the hard work, we feel that the prize is too cheap. We are motivated by mystery, drawn to the journey of detection.

This is how Paul sees the search for God in his creation. The picture is of a deductive process. From what has been made, it is possible to work out what God is like. Understanding takes time and effort. God is there for those who will look for him, but he leaves some of the work for us to do.

Continental

The only place where success comes before work is in a dictionary.

Coffee

Dear God, I love a good thriller – tracking the clues; following the path of deduction and detection; letting intuition guide me. I commit myself this day, in the world that you have made and given, to the hard work of understanding your character.

Orange Juice

For although they knew God, they neither glorified him as God nor gave thanks to him, but their thinking became futile and their foolish hearts were darkened.

ROMANS 1:21 NIV

PRIME SUSPECT

The Big Breakfast

Paul is convinced about the presence of God in the world – so convinced that he finds it hard to believe that anyone could miss it. In the mystery of creation, God is the Prime Suspect – everything points to him.

But even those who have seen the evidence can be drawn to the wrong verdict. Like the jury in a miscarriage of justice, there are those who see all that God has made, who look directly at his very fingerprints, and yet conclude that he is not there.

For Paul, this can never be the conclusion that flows naturally from the evidence – it is a choice we make. In his view, we do not begin in darkness, looking for the light of God. We begin with the light that God has given. Those who walk in darkness do so, he argues, because they have made a choice to turn off that light. For reasons of their own, they hit the dark-switch. Belief, not unbelief, is the default setting of the creation.

Continental

Just as belief and faith bring light, so unbelief brings its own kind of darkness.

Coffee

God of light and life, shine your light upon me. Scatter the darkness before my path this day. May I ever choose to walk in your light.

Orange Juice

Although they claimed to be wise, they became fools and exchanged the glory of the immortal God for images made to look like mortal man and birds and animals and reptiles.

ROMANS 1:22-23 NIV

BONE IDOL

The Big Breakfast

The battle that runs through the whole of the Old Testament – and is brought here by Paul into the New – is the battle of God versus idols. The worship of the one God, Creator of all, was constantly challenged in Hebrew history by the worship of idols – mini-gods singled out from the creation itself.

This is the irony of God's vulnerability. In his overwhelming desire to come close to us, he has given us created objects of surpassing beauty and majesty – objects that reflect his character, but on a human scale. He gives us things he knows we will like. But we reward him by making those objects themselves our idols. We worship the gift and not the Giver.

Idolatry comes about when anything God has given is made absolute – whether it is animals and birds, or wealth and power. Everything in the creation can be used as a means toward the worship of God, but anything that becomes the end in itself is an idol. When the objects of our lives become the objects of our worship, our grasp on God is diminished.

Continental

To worship is to ascribe worth – to attribute ultimate value. The idols of our culture and lives are those things that we deem ultimately worthwhile – and money, sex and power account for most of them!

Coffee

Worship belongs to you alone, our God. Praise is due to your name only. Where I have fixed my affections on gods that are no gods at all, forgive me, and receive the rightful worship of my heart.

Orange Juice
Therefore God gave them over in the sinful desires of their hearts to sexual impurity for the degrading of their bodies with one another.

ROMANS 1:24 NIV

IDEAS HAVE LEGS

The Big Breakfast
There is a popular caricature of the believer, and indeed of Paul, in which he begins to salivate with excitement at the judgement of others. His greatest pleasure is to describe the sinfulness of pleasure. A Christian is defined, in this view, as someone who is 'haunted by the terrible fear that somebody, somewhere, might be enjoying themselves.'

But difficult as these verses may be, this is a misrepresentation of their meaning. What Paul is saying, in essence, is that 'ideas have legs' – that they take you somewhere. What begins as belief flows into behaviour. If you misconstrue the intentions of the Creator, you will misuse the creation, including your own body.

There *is* a degrading side to human behaviour – and to human sexuality. Ask the victim of abuse, or the prostitute forced by poverty and circumstance to sell orgasms to strangers, or the child drawn into the dark web of paedophile exploitation. We don't like to think it of ourselves, but we are capable of the darkest of thoughts and actions.

Continental
There are two dangers in our approach to human sin. The first is to see darkness and degradation in every act – but the second is to pretend that there is no darkness in us at all.

Coffee
Creator God, we do harm to ourselves and to one another when we let the dark side of our nature hold sway. Give us the courage and strength to walk in the light.

Orange Juice
They exchanged the truth of God for a lie, and worshipped and served created things rather than the Creator – who is for ever praised. Amen.

ROMANS 1:25 NIV

THE COSMIC
RATINGS WAR

The Big Breakfast
When competing TV companies seek to assess their relative popularity, they look at two figures: total audience and audience share. They want to know how many TV sets are switched on at a given moment and, of these, how many are tuned to their programmes.

But imagine if TV sets had no off-switch; if they remained on, tuned to *something*, day and night. There would be no neutral sets to discard: audience share would be everything.

This is the picture that Paul paints of worship. Human beings are created for worship, just as we are created for love. There is no off-switch. Worship flows naturally from us to whatever object we make absolute. The screens of our lives are never blank. They broadcast our worship day and night. It is not a matter of *whether* we worship but of *what* we worship.

If you don't serve God, you will serve other gods. In the cosmic ratings war, if you are not tuned in to God's signals, you are watching something else.

Continental
It has been said that those who stop believing in God may set out to believe in nothing, but end up believing in anything.

Coffee
On the screen of my life, let the worship of God be seen day and night. On the screen of my life, let the name of God get all the credit. On the screen of my life, may God and God alone receive my praise.

Orange Juice

Jesus replied, 'Do you see these huge buildings? They will certainly be torn down! Not one stone will be left in place.'

MARK 13:2

TRABANTS AND TEMPLES

The Big Breakfast

We live in times of intense social change. Look at how far away even a recent era can seem:

Continental

What is changing – and what is constant – in your life today?

Even the much-heralded, sex-drenched 1960s look like a real dump in retrospect: cars stank, people didn't take care of their bodies, photocopiers resembled Trabants and just try finding a push-button phone to enter your answering machine's access code. Ugghh.

(From Douglas Coupland's short story, 'The Past Sucks', 1995.)

The frantic, headlong pace of change should help us to understand the strange words of Jesus in Mark 13, where the talk is of crumbling temples, earthquakes and wars – and pregnant women fleeing for the hills. Jesus uses such graphic imagery because he sees change ahead and wants his followers to be in no doubt as to where their security lies – not in the religious splendour of Judaism, nor in the military power of Rome, but in the person and words of Christ. 'The sky and the earth' (and photocopiers and answering machines …) 'will not last for ever,' Jesus says, 'but my words will'

(MARK 13:31).

Coffee

You are among us, O LORD, and we bear your name; do not forsake us!

(JEREMIAH 14:9 NIV)

Orange Juice
Shout it aloud, do not hold back. Raise your voice like a trumpet.

ISAIAH 58:1 NIV

THERE'S EVERY NEED TO SHOUT

The Big Breakfast
The depth of suffering and need in our world is vast. It is easy to become, in the words of the Canadian singer Bruce Cockburn, 'paralysed in the face of it all'. We stand in the face of an ocean of need and wonder what difference our small splash could possibly make.

For many of us, the paralysis becomes permanent and we sink into inaction, pursuing a Christian faith that has a lot to do with church and singing, and very little to do with the real needs of those who suffer.

But Isaiah, at the very outset of his Manifesto for Revival, offers us hope. Even if you can't *do* very much, you can shout, he says. You have a voice: you can raise it. And every voice, no matter how insignificant, can become in the hands of God a rallying cry. For the Hebrews, a public trumpet call was the equivalent of an air-raid siren – it stopped people in their tracks.

Use your voice, Isaiah says. Change begins when you say what you see.

Continental
Throughout the Bible, there is an emphasis on the power, for good or ill, of words. Here, Isaiah sees words, and our ability to use them, as a powerful weapon we can use on behalf of the poor.

Coffee
God of justice and peace, sometimes you whisper, and sometimes you raise your voice to make me hear. Teach me, in my own life, when it is right to stay silent, and when it is right to shout.

Orange Juice
You cannot fast as you do today and expect your voice to be heard on high.

ISAIAH 58:4 NIV

THE FAST SHOW

The Big Breakfast
Isaiah faced a generation that knew all about religious observance. Like the Pharisees in Jesus' day, they knew how to put on a show. Praying, singing, fasting and public displays of humility were all in their lexicon of spiritual performance.

Unlike other generations in the history of Israel, they were not slow to admit their need of God. They knew they stood in need of the renewing presence of God. It was the behavioural dimension of faith that they were less sure of. Reducing Judaism to rituals and public actions, they continued, outside the sphere of public religion, to flaunt God's laws. In the way they did business, in the way they dealt with conflicts and differences of opinion, in the way they treated slaves and workers, they paid no heed to the laws of God.

Religion they knew. Private morality they understood. But public justice was a foreign language to them. It is not difficult to see how many of us – in part or in full – fit much the same profile today.

Continental
Prayer without praxis is pretence; worship without works is wasted. The call of God is to obedience – in every sphere of life.

Coffee
God of Isaiah and of Jesus, you send prophets to call your people back to faith. Raise up prophets in our generation – and when they come, give us the courage to listen.

Orange Juice
Is not this the kind of fasting I have chosen: to loose the chains of injustice and untie the cords of the yoke, to set the oppressed free and break every yoke?

ISAIAH 58:6 NIV

FAST FORWARD

The Big Breakfast
In contrast to the outwardly impressive fasts of the religious Hebrews, Isaiah paints a radical picture of a different kind of fasting. Like an expert surgeon, he takes a scalpel to the world-view of his peers. He forges a dynamic link that is entirely new to them – between the 'spiritual' and the behavioural dimensions of faith.

'It is an act of prayer,' he says, 'to obey. It is an act of worship to seek justice.' Worship that pleases God is not about words and music and religious observance – it is about lives of obedience that bring the will of God to the earth. The liberation of the oppressed is a celebration of the God of Israel. Feeding the hungry is feasting on God. Loving my neighbour is an act of worship.

Isaiah goes on to outline the areas in which action is required. Spiritual disciplines are tough and take years to master, and so will lifestyle change! This is not an easier way, but a better way – and it is God's way.

Continental
Fasting is easy to understand, but hard to do. Justice is exactly the same. We find it easy to understand and explain the need for justice, but harder by far to deliver it.

Coffee
Teach us, Creator God, to offer the obedience of our daily lives and the liberation of the poor as acts of sacrifice and praise.

Orange Juice

Is it not to share your food with the hungry and to provide the poor wanderer with shelter – when you see the naked, to clothe him …

ISAIAH 58:7 NIV

OPPORTUNITY KNOCKS

The Big Breakfast

There is a hugely important clause in the challenge that Isaiah presents – it is the phrase, 'When you see …' So often, our objection to taking action for the poor comes from our sense of being overwhelmed. There are so many needs, so many causes, so many people we *could* reach out to. We don't know where to start – so we don't start at all.

Isaiah heads the objection off at the pass – you start, he says, with what you see. Before you even begin to go looking for needs, deal with the needs that are right in front of you. Who do you see, day by day – even moment by moment? Whose life could be changed by your intervention?

Like all great projects, the liberation of the planet's poor starts small. The small acts, whether offered to neighbour or stranger, will often spark off a chain reaction of obedience. Before you know it, you really will be making a difference. Don't worry, for now, about the finishing tape. Worry about getting off the starting-blocks.

Continental

A church leader who had often seen miraculous provision when those in need came to his door was once asked why he thought such 'God appointments' happened to him so often. 'God has to know he can trust you,' he replied, 'before he will give the poor your address.'

Coffee

God of the poor, God of liberation, give me the eyes to see those you are bringing to me, and the courage to act on what I see.

Orange Juice
… and not to turn away from your own flesh and blood?

ISAIAH 58:7 NIV

HE AIN'T HEAVY ...

The Big Breakfast
In my youth, a favoured form of transportation was hitch-hiking. Even when I was, for a time, the Personnel Manager of a very respectable Bristol department store, I often made the journey to and from my home in Bath by the use of my thumb. It was cheaper than the train, and sometimes faster.

On the days when it didn't go so well, I would stand by the side of a rush-hour street watching hundreds – even thousands – of cars go by, not one of their drivers paying any attention to me. On occasions I would ask myself how differently I would fare if one of the drivers recognized me. What if a member of my family was driving by? The answer, of course, is that they would stop for me – because I would no longer be a stranger in a suit incongruously commuting by hitch-hiking. I would be family – and that makes all the difference.

Those who suffer, Isaiah cries, are your own flesh and blood – it is your human family that is in need. How can you turn away?

Continental
How different would your life be if you saw those in need – from famine victims on your TV screen to *Big Issue* sellers on the street – as *family*?

Coffee
Father, I confess that, like others, I have divided humanity into 'relatives' and 'strangers'. Help me to extend the privileges of family to *all* those you bring across my path.

Orange Juice

Then your light will shine like the dawning sun, and you will quickly be healed. Your honesty will protect you as you advance, and the glory of the LORD will defend you from behind.

ISAIAH 58:8

RECIPE FOR REVIVAL!

The Big Breakfast

There are suprisingly few biblical passages that speak of the type of experience that the contemporary Church might call *revival*. Isaiah 58 is one of the few. It captures something of the hunger, the longing for God's blessing. It offers compelling and intriguing pictures of what that blessing might mean. And it offers a reliable, tried-and-tested, God-backed route *into* that blessing.

The surprising fact, for those who associate revival more with increased prayer, is that the key given here is *obedience*, not prayer. These people had prayed and fasted. They had even organized nationwide days of repentance and supplication. When it came to asking God for revival, they were up there with the best of us. But they were ignoring the poor. Their words were many – their actions few. And it wasn't enough.

Perhaps there are times when God's switchboard is so jammed with the cries of the poor that our petty calls for blessing don't get through.

Continental

When we cry for God to act – when we long for his blessing – are these times when action, not supplication, is the key?

Coffee

Many are the words we speak; many are the songs we sing; many kinds of offering – now to live the life!
(Worship leader Matt Redman)

Orange Juice
Then you will call, and the LORD will answer; you will cry for help, and he will say: Here am I.

ISAIAH 58:9 NIV

HOTLINE TO HEAVEN

The Big Breakfast
There is a circle that Isaiah closes with this phrase. His challenge to Israel has begun with the assertion that prayer alone will not suffice – that words empty of action are words empty of effect. Back up your words with obedience – match your passionate prayer-style with a compassionate lifestyle – and God will hear you, the prophet says.

He also goes further. The obedience he cries for will open up the channels of communication with God. Compassionate action will increase your knowledge of God. Having abandoned the insufficiency of words to embrace obedience, you will return to a prayer-life that is revitalized with meaning and effectiveness. You will enjoy the best of both worlds.

Obedience is the key that sparks the ignition system of prayer.

Continental
It is not for lack of passion or commitment that prayer becomes dust-dry. It is for lack of action. Take the action – make the change – and see how your prayers come to life.

Coffee
Father God, I dare not force a choice between passion in prayer and compassion in life – I dare to ask for both. Fill my actions with your love, and my prayers with your presence.

Orange Juice
If you do away with the yoke of oppression, with the pointing finger and malicious talk …

ISAIAH 58:9 NIV

WAR OF THE WORDS

The Big Breakfast
Having established that words without action have no power in prayer, Isaiah now turns to the very real power that words *do* have – the power to oppress. If you are going to do away with oppression, he says, you will need to watch what you say. Talk has power: oppression includes what we do with our words.

There is wisdom of the deepest kind here. How often we see racism begin with language. How often those who speak ill of their enemies later act ill toward them. Those who lived in Croatia and Serbia in the early 1990s, in the months leading up to the horrors of war, have testified that what eventually happened on the battlefield happened first in the media – and in everyday conversation.

It is easier to kill and maim those you have already spoken of as worthless. Violent words are seeds for violent acts. To be rid of oppression, you must strike at the very root – the tongue.

Continental
Most of us are not guilty of physical violence towards those around us – but how many of us are guilty of verbal GBH?

Coffee
For the violence that uses neither guns nor fists, but arms the tongue with fire, *Father, forgive us.* For the oppression that knows no locks or bars, but imprisons its victims with words, *Father, forgive us.*

Orange Juice

… and if you spend yourselves on behalf of the hungry and satisfy the needs of the oppressed, then your light will rise in the darkness, and your night will become like the noonday.

ISAIAH 58:10 NIV

REVERSAL OF FORTUNE

The Big Breakfast

Fridge doors used to be there for paintings brought home from play-school and for scribbled shopping-lists. Not any more. It is now possible to buy themed collections of magnetic words from which to fashion all manner of creative writing – from love-letters and poetry to household messages: 'Your dinner's in the dog.'

Imagine that you had such a word-set made up of the language of 21st-Century advertising. From the slogans bombarding us each day, you might construct a common message: 'Spend all you have on yourself, until *your* needs are satisfied.'

Now imagine that Isaiah comes to call. You leave him alone in the kitchen for a few moments, and before you know it he has messed with the words to turn the message round. With a subtle change of word order, he has switched the polarity on consumer culture: 'Don't spend *on* yourself, but spend *yourself*. And don't stop spending until the needs of the oppressed are met.' It is with such simple words that revolutions are constructed.

Continental

What would the impact be if you started to keep track of your spending *of* yourself as closely as you track your spending *on* yourself?

Coffee

Dear God, I enjoy spending. I take pleasure in the anticipation of buying something for myself. It is one of the things that most satisfies me. Help me, selfless God, to spend myself with equal joy.

Orange Juice

The LORD will always guide you and provide good things to eat when you are in the desert. He will make you healthy. You will be like a garden that has plenty of water or like a stream that never runs dry.

ISAIAH 58:11

GROUND FORCE

The Big Breakfast

A recent trend in broadcasting is programmes offering home and garden transformations – in the UK *Changing Rooms* and *Ground Force* are just two examples of the genre.

We love these shows because we believe that our homes and gardens can and should reflect our prosperity and status. By implication, we establish a graduating scale of abundance. The successful will have designer interiors. The *really* successful will have designer interiors *and* landscaped gardens. And the really super-successful will have designer interiors and landscaped gardens with a water-feature!

But all of this is not as new as we may think. In Isaiah's day the same was true – there was no image of abundance and fruitfulness more perfect than that of a well-watered garden. The longing, then as now, was for Eden restored. The image is used here as a graphic promise: the selfless compassion of this chapter will not lead to want and misery, but to an abundance of life beyond imagining. Live this way, and God will give your life a *Ground Force* make-over!

Continental

If you picture your life as a garden, what kind of garden is it? What would you ask the *Ground Force* team to change?

Coffee

Creator, Father of all, you give me life, you give me love, you give me yourself. Help me to give my life, my love, myself to you.
(David Adam)

Orange Juice
You will rebuild those houses left in ruins for years; you will be known as a builder and repairer of city walls and streets.

ISAIAH 58:12

BOB THE BUILDER

The Big Breakfast
Isaiah was not called to address the unchurched so much as the over-churched. The ruins – the leftovers – of God's past glories surrounded the people of Israel. They had enough of the lingering memory of God from the past to inoculate them against his action in the present – but not enough to shake them into worship.

Isaiah's words are doubly meaningful in the context of contemporary Western culture, in which we are surrounded, often literally, by ruined churches. Is there hope, in the post-Christian West, for renewal? Is it possible to rebuild on the very ground on which the Church once stood, and has failed?

For Isaiah, the answer is yes. Our God is the God of the second chance, the God of new beginnings. In every age, with every new generation, he holds out the twin offer of reformation and renewal. But the key is obedience – a return not to the form of religion, but to the reality within it. Rebuilders start their work by getting back to foundations. Can he fix it? Yes he can!

Continental
There are times when rebuilding begins with demolition: what is left of the old must be torn down, so that the new can be built on its foundations.

Coffee
We cannot be born anew until the old has died within us.
(From Paul Tillich, *The Shaking of the Foundations*)

Orange Juice
But first, you must start respecting the Sabbath as a joyful day of worship. You must stop doing and saying whatever you please on this special day.

ISAIAH 58:13

JUST ANOTHER MANIC SUNDAY?

The Big Breakfast
Isaiah 58 is the prototypical Freedom Song. It speaks of liberation for the oppressed; of abundance for the poor; of new life for the masses. It is as close as the Bible gets to flying a Red Flag and hitting the streets for a revolution.

So it is incongruous, to the 21st-Century mind, that the chapter ends on the Sabbath. Sabbath observance, to us, is about legalism – about a view of religion that is anything but liberating.

But Isaiah knows what he is about. God's Law, exemplified in the rules of the Sabbath, is all about freedom. It is the Sabbath that tells the employer that he cannot own his workers body and soul – nor, for that matter, his slaves, animals or land. No matter how caught up we become in our get-rich schemes, there is a time when God says 'Enough!' and we must take our hands off.

Every part of the creation – from atoms to empires – must be allowed rest and recovery. Our exploitation of the earth is limited by design. God's cry of 'Time out!' is also a cry of freedom.

Continental
Sabbath-rest is good news for the poor: it is the powerful who are constrained and limited by it.

Coffee
God of Sabbath-rest, teach me today what it means to rest in you. Grant to all those who are wearied by labour and struggle the rest that you alone can provide.

Orange Juice

… then you will find your joy in the LORD, and I will cause you to ride on the heights of the land and to feast on the inheritance of your father Jacob.

ISAIAH 58:14 NIV

YOU'LL GET WHAT'S COMING TO YOU!

The Big Breakfast

The abundance that the prophet Isaiah foresees for those who obey God is no less than the blessings promised to Jacob. From the very beginnings of time, God has been looking to bless his creatures.

There are promises to Eve and Adam; to Abraham and Sarah; to Noah and Moses and Jacob; to Ruth and David and Solomon and Deborah. The story of God's dealings with women and men is pregnant with his blessings. With every character, with every incident, the weight of the promise intensifies, like water building up behind a dam.

Discover the way of obedience, Isaiah is saying, and you will breach the dam. The blessing of God is not a meal but a feast. It is not a trickle but a flood. His intention is not to tickle you with small mercies, but to knock you off your feet. The longing of the creation for the blessings of God is matched by the longing of the Creator to bless. The key – the bridge between the two – is the obedience of the people of God.

Continental

The whole creation is waiting, Paul says – longing in desperate expectation – for the people of God to come into their inheritance.

Coffee

God of Eve and Adam, who walked with you in Eden – *Let your promise be fulfilled in our age.* God of Abraham and Sarah, whose longings were turned to laughter – *Let your promise be fulfilled in our age.*

Orange Juice

Straight away the cock crowed a second time. Then Peter remembered that Jesus had told him, 'Before a cock crows twice you will say three times that you don't know me.' So Peter started crying.

MARK 14:72

THE BIRTH OF A LEADER

The Big Breakfast

With the arrest of Jesus, the fast-paced narrative of Mark's Gospel hits breakneck velocity. If this were a movie, the music would be hard and driving, and the camera would cut from scene to scene with dizzying intensity.

In the middle of this tumbling drama Peter's denial emerges as a turning-point in the whole epic. Jesus has had just three years to prepare a group of disciples to carry on his kingdom work. He has already chosen Peter as their leader. But Peter is still not ready. There is too much pride in him; too much self-reliance; too much impetuous activism.

Jesus has gone – he will not speak to Peter again this side of resurrection. But here at last, in a cold, dark courtyard in the frozen moments before dawn, Peter reaches an end of himself. The time-bomb of Jesus' words predicting denial explodes, and Peter's pride is broken. He weeps uncontrollably – and in that moment, as in no other, Pentecost and the birth of the Church become possible.

Continental

It was not Peter's weakness that got in the way, but his strength. It may be the gifts we have, not the gifts we lack, that block the purposes of God in our lives.

Coffee

Thirty years later Peter wrote: 'Humble yourselves, therefore, under God's mighty hand, that he may lift you up in due time.'
(1 Peter 5:6–7 NIV)

Orange Juice

Tax collectors and sinners were all crowding round to listen to Jesus. The Pharisees and the teachers of the Law of Moses started grumbling, 'This man is friendly with sinners. He even eats with them.'

LUKE 15:1-2

THE WELCOME WAGON

The Big Breakfast

Christian tradition paints the Pharisees as the pantomime baddies of the Gospel narratives. Wherever Jesus went, we imagine, cries of 'They're behind you!' would alert him to a slapstick gaggle of Pharisees, out to trip him up.

We see these men as small-minded, mean-spirited, selfish – the conspiratorial enemies of Christ. The truth is less comic, and more complex. Pharisees were committed, consistent, single-minded. Their focus was on the things of God, and their willingness to apply their faith to the tiniest detail of daily life was extraordinary. The zeal that consumed them was zeal for Israel's God.

What set them at loggerheads with Jesus, and vice versa, was this – they had forgotten the character of the God on whom they focused so much zeal. Desire for God had hardened into the dogma by which desire was quenched. The search for truth became a system by which truth was suppressed.

Church history shows us just how easy it is for those who believe to become those who suppress belief – for followers to become Pharisees.

Continental

Unlike the Pharisees, the tax collectors and 'sinners' gathered to hear Jesus. What was it about Jesus that made him so attractive to ordinary people?

Coffee

Reflect on your meal-times of recent weeks – how often have you been willing to break bread with 'the wrong sort of people'?

Orange Juice
Then Jesus told them this story: 'If any of you has a hundred sheep and one of them gets lost…'

LUKE 15:3–4

ALIEN NATION

The Big Breakfast
In our day, a shepherd might be tempted to respond to Jesus' question with a shrugged 'fair enough'. A one per cent loss on the initial investment is not the end of the world – it's probably better to keep the 99 safe than to risk all searching for the one that was stupid enough to get lost. Why not just accept that this is 'the survival of the fittest'? That's without even beginning to think of insurance.

We have so immunized ourselves against loss that the odd sheep dead or dying really doesn't matter. How else can we tolerate the loss of six million lives each year to starvation; the recruitment of over 80 million children worldwide into the slavery of child labour; the death of 40,000 children every hour from preventable diseases?

By contrast, God's view of loss is extravagant and outrageous – he will go to the ends of the earth to prevent the suffering of just one human being. There is no loss adjustment in the kingdom of heaven – just the extravagance of a 99-to-1-risk-taking God.

Continental
How would your life change if you took on a Godly intolerance of the lostness that you witness every day?

Coffee
Alienation … is an ache in the deepest part of you, a longing which nothing in the world ever quite touches … the sense of being lost comes like a fragment of a song … Finding the way is all about coming home.
(From Mike Riddell, *Godzone – A Guide to the Travels of the Soul*, Lion, 1992)

Orange Juice
Jesus continued: 'There was a man who had two sons …'

LUKE 15:11 NIV

IN THE BEGINNING ...

The Big Breakfast
Many of the parables of Jesus begin with the phrase, 'There was a man who' – a man who planted a vineyard; who had two sons; who went on a journey. In almost every case what is offered is a picture of God.

For Jesus, every story begins with God – the God who exists already; who has made the world in which we live; who seeks to know us and walk with us; whose only longing is to father and mother us. According to Jesus, philosophy and theology do not begin with a blank sheet of paper, nor indeed with the details of our own experience, but with the person of God our Maker. Every story – the story of the universe and the story of each of us within it – begins with the creative, generous, merciful personality of God.

How strange that we have tried so hard to write our history without him – as if it were possible to understand the cosmos without reference to the one, colossal presence by which it is filled.

Continental
Both the Old and New Testaments in places use female, motherly images of God. What might it mean for you to embrace not only the fathering but also the mothering of God?

Coffee
With the story of the lost son fresh in your mind, pray through the Lord's Prayer *(Matthew 6:9–13)*, and ask God to help you see how your story – your life – begins with his choice to parent you.

Orange Juice

The younger one said to his father, 'Give me my share of the property.' So the father divided his property between his two sons.

LUKE 15:12

DROP DEAD, DAD!

The Big Breakfast

The shock of this story is the audacity of the younger son. By asking to cash in his inheritance early, he is wishing his father dead. In saying, 'I want it all, and I want it now,' he is saying to the father who has loved and raised him, 'Our relationship means nothing to me – you're worth more to me dead than alive.'

When I was a sharp-tongued teenager ready to express my own pain by inflicting verbal pain on others, I had a youth leader who would give me a withering look and say, 'You know how to hurt.'

The son in the story knew how to hurt his father – to reject him at the deepest possible level. And sure enough, once the bank draft had been cashed, he put physical space where the emotional chasm had grown, and was gone.

If this is a picture of God's dealings with us, then it offers a compelling insight into the way God *feels* towards us. It's not the money – the quantitative measure of our so-called 'sins' – that matters most, but the broken relationship.

Continental

The most hurtful thing that can come between you and God is distance.

Coffee

God my Father, swallow up the distance that has come between us. Draw near, I pray, in the passing moments of this day.

Orange Juice

Not long after that, the younger son got together all he had, set off for a distant country …

LUKE 15:13 NIV

ANOTHER COUNTRY

The Big Breakfast

We are told nothing of the country to which the boy travelled – only that it was 'a distant country'. The implication is twofold.

Firstly, he wanted to put some miles between himself and his father. He did not just dislike living at home – he despised it. He was determined that his spending spree would be well away from the watchful eyes of his family.

Secondly, he wanted to try his luck in a new situation. The fact that there were pig farms in this land indicates that it was not only *distant* from Israel but *different* as well. Farming pigs, handling pigs, being with pigs would all be unacceptable activities to a devout Jew.

Along with spurning his family, the son was rejecting faith and tradition. He was voting with his feet to opt out of the community that had nurtured him – though the substitute community that he joined was insincere and short-lived. Whatever else the son's actions reveal, they reveal the desire to get as far away as possible from everything the father stood for. Whatever he became, he wanted to be his own person.

Continental

The story of the lost son contains movement away from the father, and movement once again towards the father. Which of these is most strongly present in your life?

Coffee

Take a few moments to pray for those you know whose search for identity has led them to 'a distant country'.

Orange Juice

... where he wasted all his money in wild living.

LUKE 15:13

REBEL WITHOUT APPLAUSE

The Big Breakfast

This parable shows a remarkable understanding of the workings of rebellion – and is not entirely unsympathetic to this younger son. There is a world out there to explore, and the call of the new and unfamiliar is strong.

Continental
Success may be a good companion – but failure is by far the better teacher.

Some of us are able to accept the faith and values of our elders at face value – others of us find that we have to tear it up to see what it's made of. Rebellion, in some hands, is an act of self-discovery – a step along the road to maturity. The good news of this story is that rebellion is not the end of the road.

Jesus doesn't once express judgement of the younger son – he leaves his listeners to make up their own minds – but by the end of the story the younger son is in a better place than his brother is.

It's your destination that matters, not the route you take to get there. Your journey might take in some distant countries – and even some places of famine and hardship – but the key is to know that, through it all, your ultimate direction is homeward.

Coffee

I prefer a person who has sinned if he knows he has sinned and has repented, over a person who has not sinned and considers himself to be righteous.
(From Abba Sarnatus of the Desert Fathers, quoted in *Celtic Daily Prayer*, Marshall Pickering, London, 1994)

Orange Juice
He would have been glad to eat what the pigs were eating, but nobody gave him a thing.

LUKE 15:16

ALL YOU LOVE
IS NEED

The Big Breakfast
There is a story told of Prince Charles visiting a shelter for the homeless in London. He stopped for a while to speak with one man of about his own age – a man who had been living on the streets for several years.

The man gave his name and waited for a glimmer of recognition. When none came, he revealed that he had known the Prince in his youth, when they had been at school together. Companions in childhood, they had grown to live in two different worlds – the one enriched by wealth and power, the other destroyed by alcohol.

For the lost son in the parable, the symbol of the depth of his fall was at his feet, in the pigswill he was forbidden to eat. The son of a landowner and a child of Israel, he had hit rock bottom and he knew it. It took desperation – a hunger that was at once physical, emotional and spiritual – to bring him to his senses. The worst thing that happened to him was also the best, because it woke him up.

Continental
'Pain,' said C. S. Lewis, 'is God's megaphone to rouse a deaf world.'

Coffee
When in your life has God used desperation to bring you to your senses? Do you resent the pain – or can you see it for what it was and thank him?

Orange Juice

Finally, he came to his senses and said, 'My father's workers have plenty to eat, and here I am, starving to death!'

LUKE 15:17

AMNESIACS ANONYMOUS

The Big Breakfast

Hunger brought the boy to his senses, but it took something more to bring him home. In the midst of his disgust and degradation, there was something he remembered – a lost fragment from his childhood – which both challenged him to go home, and gave him the courage to do so.

He had wished his father dead. He had run from him as far as he could go. He had sought peace and prosperity where they couldn't be found. Finally, he was reduced to working as a hired labourer for a man who paid him so badly that he couldn't afford to eat – and refused to give him even pig slops.

And that's when the penny dropped – in all his years growing up alongside the father he so despised, he had never once seen him treat a worker that way. Even without pigs, on his dad's farm there were men doing the same kind of dirty, degrading work as he was now doing – but they weren't ill treated and hungry.

It was a recovered memory that drove him home – the memory of his father's generosity.

Continental

For a culture on the run from its Creator, as much as for the individual, the way home begins with remembering the generosity of God.

Coffee

Reawaken in my life, O God, the memory of your love. Bring to my mind this day the generous reality of Jesus.

Orange Juice
The elder son had been out in the field. But when he came near the house, he heard the music and dancing.

LUKE 15:25

BIG BROTHER IS WATCHING YOU

The Big Breakfast
It should have been the end of the story. Prodigal son returns, is reconciled to prodigal father … prodigal celebration ensues. But it wasn't to be.

Right from the start, this has been the story not of one son but of two. Bitterness, jealousy, ingratitude and anger all flood out as Big Brother hears of the return and sees his father's reaction. Like his brother, he has forgotten the generosity of his father – but he has done so without moving to a far country.

He has stayed with his father, working for him, living cheek by jowl with him – and yet his familiarity has bred not contentment but contempt. A slow distance has grown between father and son, until the gulf is as wide as ever it was for the younger brother.

This is a story of two lost sons – the first lost in arrogance, rebellion and the lusts of youth, the second lost in religion and conformity. Only the first, in Jesus' telling, finds his way home.

Continental
The tragedy of religion – the great, aching pain at the heart of the Church – is that it is possible, like this son, to be obedient, compliant, faithful – and yet end up in bitterness and anger.

Coffee
Henri J. Nouwen, in *The Return of the Prodigal Son*, finds traces in his own life of both the younger son and the older son. Is this true for you?

Orange Juice
The elder brother got so angry that he would not even go into the house … he said to his father, 'For years I have worked for you like a slave … but you have never even given me a little goat, so that I could give a dinner for my friends.'

LUKE 15:28-29

IT'S HIS PARTY BUT I'LL CRY IF I WANT TO ...

The Big Breakfast
There is an intriguing detail in the drama of the story – revealing the gritty realism of Jesus the storyteller.

All the anger of the older brother, his years of disappointment and bitterness, his genuine sense of hurt at being snubbed by his father – all this finds its focus on the fattened calf. The return of the brother is the issue – but it is the celebration that brings out the anger.

Like his listeners, Jesus has grown up in an ordinary family. He knows that if a row is going to erupt, it will erupt during a party. Weddings, funerals, anniversary celebrations – such family gatherings are the best possible catalyst for long-held feelings of jealousy and anger to break the surface.

The son's homecoming was not the first party in history to be destroyed by sibling rivalry – and it probably won't be the last!

Continental
It is tragic when resentment arises in a family – but more tragic by far to let it grow unexpressed over years until it builds to breaking-point.

Coffee
Are you in relationships in which resentment and bitterness have taken root? Don't wait for the next fattened calf to be slaughtered – deal with it now!

Orange Juice

'…But when this son of yours who has squandered your property with prostitutes comes home, you kill the fattened calf for him!'

'My son,' the father said. '…this brother of yours was dead and is alive again; he was lost and is found.

LUKE 15:30–31 NIV

WATCH YOUR LANGUAGE!

The Big Breakfast

The brother's anger manifests itself in grammar. The servant tells him, 'Your brother has come,' but when he speaks to his father, his brother is 'this son of *yours*'. Language betrays the depth of feeling.

It is the father who has been wronged and rejected – and yet it is the older brother who keeps the offence alive. He really has no grievance against his brother – but he uses the younger son's irresponsibility as a vehicle for his own frustrations. His response is to present his father with a choice – 'It's you and me or you and him.'

But the father will have none of it. *His* language is the language of reconciliation – 'We had to celebrate because *this brother of yours* is alive again.'

How often do we try to maintain a relationship with our Father whilst breaking a relationship with a brother or sister? God's desire is for reconciliation – not only between child and parent, but amongst children too.

Continental

Love is like a television picture – there's no point in having the vertical hold adjusted if the horizontal hold is out of control.

Coffee

As you speak to God, be aware that when you pray using such words as 'this son of yours', he will often reply in terms of 'this brother of yours'.

Orange Juice

The chief priests brought many charges against Jesus. The Pilate questioned him again, 'Don't you have anything to say? Don't you hear what crimes they say you have done?' But Jesus did not answer, and Pilate was amazed.

MARK 15:3-5

YOU SAY IT BEST WHEN YOU SAY NOTHING AT ALL

The Big Breakfast

For the most part, Jesus is remembered for the things he said. There are certain moments, though, which have significance not for what was said but for what was not said.

Standing before Pilate, it is not the eloquence of Christ that speaks volumes but his silence. It is not that Jesus is afraid of verbal conflict, or that he has no answer for his accusers. On other occasions, he has engaged in lengthy and complex debate with these very men. He is silent because a greater purpose is at work.

The powerlessness to which he surrenders himself is also wordlessness – he will not use the weapon of his tongue in his own defence, nor allow himself the satisfaction of a well-aimed verbal missile. In his silence is a personal power by which even Pilate is confounded.

Months earlier, Christ's disciples had said to him, 'You have the words of eternal life.' On this occasion they might equally have said, 'You have the silence of eternal life.'

Continental

Religions of the East and ancient Christianity alike make creative use of silence in prayer. What might its recovery mean for your personal spiritual walk?

Coffee

Why not commit yourself to finding a few moments of silence today, to explore the richness of prayer without words?

Orange Juice
The LORD is my shepherd, I shall not be in want.

PSALM 23:1 NIV

UP CLOSE AND PERSONAL

The Big Breakfast
Great poet and songwriter as he was, even David had to write 22 Psalms before he had a hit! So the Broadway joke goes.

The truth is, for many people, Psalm 23 is the only Psalm – possibly the only fragment of the Bible – that they know. Its moving words and strong images have written themselves into the very heart of our culture and history – from the lifeboats of the *Titanic* to the mourners at countless funerals each day.

The miracle of this poem of worship is captured in its first five words. 'The Lord' is *Yahweh* – a Hebrew name meaning 'HE IS', derived from Moses' encounter with the 'I AM' of the burning bush. HE IS universal and unnameable, above all and over all. He cannot be pinned down to time and place. The world cannot contain him and words cannot describe him. Yet HE IS my shepherd – intimate, earthy, humble, near at hand.

If David knew anything, he knew that it took humility to be a shepherd. The God who is 'up there and unapproachable' is the same God who is up close and personal.

Continental
The God who made the world of which I am so small a part has chosen to be part of my small world.

Coffee
God my shepherd, thank you for choosing to live in my world. May any distance between us be dissolved. May I know you, up close and personal, today.

Orange Juice
He makes me lie down in green pastures, he leads me beside quiet waters …

PSALM 23:2 NIV

PASTURE EYES

The Big Breakfast
Sheep, down through the ages, have had a bad press. We think of them as stubborn and stupid. We picture them straying into danger, wandering off mountainsides. But there is one area in which the average sheep is, I confess, brighter than I am. It is this: sheep know what's good for them. The shepherd leads the sheep to food and water, and the sheep know what to do. My experience of human behaviour, including my own, is less positive.

How often do we resist the God who leads us to food, shelter, refreshment and rest? How many of our difficulties result from our stubborn refusal to accept these good gifts? What God intends as refreshment, we shirk as duty. What he offers as rest, we misinterpret as restriction. Failing to see, or to trust, the good pastures to which he is leading us, we invent an endless list of other 'needs', and press blindly for their fulfilment. We need eyes to see the perfect provision he has made for us in the place in which we stand.

Continental
When you look around at the place God has brought you to, do you begin to see the safe pastures and quiet waters you need?

Coffee
When we claim to have foresight, second sight and insight, but in reality even our first sight is short, Father, open our eyes.

Orange Juice
… he restores my soul. He guides me in paths of righteousness for his name's sake.

PSALM 23:3 NIV

JOURNEY INTO LIFE

The Big Breakfast
The concept of 'righteousness', to the Hebrew mind, has several elements. It contains the sense of moral 'rightness' – the paths on which God leads bring me into conformity to his law and will.

It also contains the dynamic of justice. 'Right living' is not simply an individual matter – it spills over into the community and the world. The paths on which God leads me will bring me into right relationship with the human and non-human creation.

Finally, 'righteousness' contains a uniquely Hebrew sense of *prosperity*. The life to which God leads me is a life of abundance and rest – life in all its fullness. To divorce this third meaning from the first two – to seek prosperity with no regard for moral truth or global justice – is to strip Psalm 23 of its meaning. A gospel written in dollar or pound signs with no place for the poor has no place in the Bible.

The path to abundance *is* the road to justice – those who claim to know a short-cut are blind guides.

Continental
There are three signposts to look for on your journey with God. The signpost of obedience calls you to conform to God's laws. The signpost of justice calls you to care for the creation and its people. The signpost of abundance calls you to enjoy the fullness of God's blessing.

Coffee
In all my dealings today, lead me, gentle Shepherd, in the ways that lead to life.

Orange Juice

Even though I walk through the valley of the shadow of death, I will fear no evil …

PSALM 23:4 NIV

SHADOW BOXING

The Big Breakfast

The language at this point is very specific – not 'the valley of death' but 'the valley of the *shadow* of death'. The physical image is of a ravine or mountain pass so deep and steep that the sun rarely hits its floor. To walk through it is to pass into shadow.

For sheep, this is a place not of danger but of fear. It is not what might happen to them that holds them back from walking this way, but what they imagine might happen. In real terms, the sheep are in more danger drinking from the quiet waters – where lions and bears are known to prowl; where their defences are down; where the shepherd is most likely to nap! But shadows have a habit of worsening fear. And sheep, like people, will hold back from shadows as much as from real dangers.

The shepherd knows that this route is both necessary and safe – and he is on his guard to keep it so. But the sheep, if they are to follow, must face their fears.

Continental

What are you most afraid of? The passages of your life that are, for you, places of shadow are the places where God most wants to walk with you.

Coffee

Father, I am driven and controlled by fear, and by the fear of fear. Deliver me, so that I may walk every path you call me to in obedience, trust and joy.

Orange Juice
… your rod and your staff, they comfort me.

PSALM 23:4 NIV

POKE, POKE, CLACK, CLACK

The Big Breakfast
The antidote to the fears that have us running from shadows is to know the presence of God.

The rod and staff remind the sheep that the shepherd has not left them to their fears. When darkness overwhelms them, and they can see neither the ground under their feet, nor their shepherd up ahead, the 'clack, clack' of staff on rock tells them they are not alone – and gives direction.

When they are paralysed by their terror, caught between a rock and a hard place and without the strength to move, the 'poke, poke' of a rod in the ribs brings them to their senses, breaking the thrall of fear.

In the dark night of the soul, when my certainties have gone down with the sun and I see monsters in the shadows on the wall, 'clack, clack, poke, poke' may well be all I know of God. But I cling to these small mercies, and listen hard.

Continental
I am safe because the shepherd has chosen this route. Though I fear the worst, and though the worst I fear may come to pass, I trust myself into his care.

Coffee
Teach me, Father, to listen for the quiet echo of your presence. Help me to recognize the imperative of your love in the shocks and pains you let me feel to save me from myself.

Orange Juice

You prepare a table before me in the presence of my enemies. You anoint my head with oil; my cup overflows.

PSALM 23:5 NIV

SLEEPING WITH THE ENEMY

The Big Breakfast

Even in its time and context, this is a bizarre image. The prayer and longing of Israel was always that they might be granted 'rest from our enemies on every side'. The sign of peace was the absence of enemies. The feast took place far from the battlefield.

But David, since his youth as a shepherd, has become a shrewd military commander. He knows well that the absence of enemies is not always the sign of peace. True victory is to triumph in the presence of one's enemies. David wants his enemies where he can see them – where he knows, once and for all, that they are no threat to him, and where they can see him.

The anointing with oil is a sign of God's vindication. The overflowing cup is the measure of his provision. God's answer to the spiritual battles you face is not to take you away from your enemies to the false peace that pretends they are not there. It is to overwhelm you, in the very presence of your foe, with the anointing and abundance of his mercy.

Continental

There are times when God delivers us *from* our troubles – more often, though, he delivers us *in* our troubles.

Coffee

My instinct, Lord God, is to run from battle. I don't like confrontation and I would rather have no enemies at all. Thank you that your plan is not flight but victory.

Orange Juice
Surely goodness and love will follow me all the days of my life …

PSALM 23:6 NIV

WAKEY WAKEY!

The Big Breakfast
Picture yourself on a cross-Channel ferry, watching the land you have left behind recede in the distance. Across the water, stretching almost to the horizon, you will see the fading trail, the wake, of the boat on which you stand. As the huge propellers plough through the sea, they churn up the water to leave this frothing, white-topped pattern behind them.

This image is something like the picture given in this Psalm. The Hebrew shepherd would always lead from the front, not from behind. Ancient shepherding was an entirely different proposition from the dog-aided cajoling of today.

But as we follow the shepherd and forge ahead, what comes behind us? For David, the miracle of God's shepherding will be seen in the goodness and mercy that follow him. In each place that he goes, on each path of righteousness on which he is led, he will leave behind the pattern of goodness and mercy. The presence of God will not only mark his life – it will also mark the places where he has been.

Continental
As you pass through your workplace, your home, your community – what do you leave in your wake?

Coffee
I am conscious, Father, that wherever I go, I leave a mark. Strengthen me, renew me, change me, so that goodness and mercy follow in my wake.

Orange Juice

... and I will dwell in the house of the LORD for ever.

PSALM 23:6 NIV

HOME, SWEET HOME

The Big Breakfast

Having explored agricultural imagery, and briefly flirted with things military, Psalm 23 ends with the most human of images: the idea of 'home'.

The 'house of the Lord' is neither a physical building nor some future, mythical paradise. It is the reality of a life lived daily in his company. To dwell in the house of the Lord is to be at home with God, to live in the immediacy of his presence and to be subject to his house-rules. If you can imagine sharing an apartment with the eternal God, then you can begin to see the intimacy being pictured here.

Let God's be the first face you see when you wake, and the last you say goodnight to. Let his preferences shape your décor, your leisure time, your shopping lists. The house of the Lord is not a building with a text from Joshua displayed in the hall – it is a life lived in the certainty of God's moment-by-moment presence. The end and aim of faith is cohabitation with the Creator.

Continental

The TV programme *Through the Keyhole* guesses at someone's identity by visiting their home. Do those who are invited into your life sense that they are in 'the house of God'?

Coffee

Thank you, Father God, that you have made it possible for me to live in your presence. Make yourself at home in my life. Thank you that the intimacy we share is not for this age alone, but will go on forever.

Orange Juice
He is the image of the invisible God …

COLOSSIANS 1:15 NIV

PORTRAIT OF THE ARTIST

The Big Breakfast
The Bible speaks of the image of God being found in three places. In Genesis, women and men are described as 'made in the image of God'. In Romans 2, the invisible qualities of God are said to be 'made visible' in what he has made – the Creator is seen in his creation.

But nowhere is the language of the Bible as specific and strong as here in Colossians. Jesus is not just *a* picture of God; he is not just somewhere to look to see something of God revealed – he is the exact likeness, the 'icon' of the invisible God. If God had a passport, Jesus would be the picture in it. If you talked to God via Web Cam, Jesus would be the face you would see.

You can learn a lot about Vincent Van Gogh from his pictures. The character of the artist comes through in his work. But it is only in a self-portrait that his physical likeness is seen. Jesus is God's self-portrait – his ultimate and final effort to let the world see what he is like.

Continental
Consider the creation. Meditate on the likeness of God in your fellow women and men. But for the whole picture, take the time to study Jesus.

Coffee
In the wonder of all that you have made, *Father, show yourself to me.* In the beauty of your creatures, women and men, *Father, show yourself to me.* In your Son Jesus, the perfect likeness of the eternal God, *Father, let me see you as you are.*

Orange Juice
... the firstborn over all creation.

COLOSSIANS 1:15 NIV

FIRST THINGS FIRST

The Big Breakfast
The firstborn son held a very privileged place in both Hebrew and Roman mythologies. He was the heir, the true successor to the father. Under the father, he held a place of authority in the family. In a patriarchal culture, he carried immense responsibility, and enjoyed privileges to match.

Paul uses this image to try and capture the uniqueness of Jesus. Jesus is the 'son and heir' of the created order – one with us, and yet above us. He is the one destined to lead the universe.

But there is more here. The firstborn also had a role in the Hebrew sacrificial system. It was the first fruits that were given back to God in the tithe. The sacrificial lamb was a firstborn lamb.

Just as God asks us to give the first and best to him, so he offers his first and best in sacrifice for us. Jesus is uniquely placed to rule the universe, and uniquely qualified to give himself for its redemption. The measure of the stature of Christ is a measure of the generosity of God.

Continental
As the 'firstborn Son', Jesus is not only the privileged ruler of the universe – he is also our big brother. In one person, the ultimate authority and the ultimate intimacy come together.

Coffee
Blessed are you, Lord Jesus Christ: King of the universe, yet born of the Virgin Mary.

Orange Juice
For by him all things were created: things in heaven and on earth, visible and invisible, whether thrones or powers or rulers or authorities; all things were created by him and for him.
COLOSSIANS 1:16 NIV

THE ARTIST OF THE PORTRAIT

The Big Breakfast
In all truth there is great paradox. The contradictions in the Bible are not the end of faith, but its beginning.

Paul has told us that Jesus is somehow part of the created order, our big brother before God. Now he wants us to know that Jesus is the Creator. He is not only the portrait of the artist, but the artist of the portrait.

This Jesus, born of a teenage mother in the blood and sweat and straw of an impoverished stable, is the same Jesus who was there when the composition of blood, and the make-up of sweat, and the genetic code of straw were all decided.

Immense is the love of the Father for the creation; more immense still is the love of the Father for the Son. Before the world came into being, there was this passion, this exchange of love between Father and Son. Jesus is both the expression and the object of the Father's love. He is the Creator, and the reason for creating. Faith in Christ begins not at Calvary but in Eden.

Continental
At every stage of salvation history, Jesus is at the centre of God's action. In creation, it is by Jesus that the world is made. In the fall, it is in Jesus that God enters into his broken world. In redemption, it is in Christ that all things find fulfilment.

Coffee
Christ the Creator, I praise you for the world that you have made. Christ Incarnate, I welcome you as brother and friend. Christ the Redeemer, I honour you as King of a universe made new.

Orange Juice
He is before all things, and in him all things hold together.

COLOSSIANS 1:17 NIV

EVERY BREATH YOU TAKE

The Big Breakfast
Jesus spans the past, present and future of the created order. In him, the verb 'created' loses its captivity to the past historic tense. It is true to say that Jesus created everything things, but it is also true that he goes on creating – holding everything together moment by moment.

To speak of God as Creator is not to describe a job he once held for six days several aeons ago; it is to speak of an ongoing dynamic relationship between the eternal God and the universe he has made.

It took science 20 centuries to catch up with this idea. Since Einstein physicists have been engaged in the search for the 'theory of everything' – the unifying principle by which the whole universe exists. Jesus is that principle – through a moment-by-moment decision of his will and love, he holds everything together.

Black holes can't bounce without Jesus. The stars can't shimmer without Jesus. Particles can't party without Jesus. You can't breathe without Jesus.

Continental
The act of creation is a 24 hours a day, 7 days a week, 52 weeks of the year ongoing declaration of God's love.

Coffee
As a star abides in the light of God, as the planets abide in the patterns set out for them, as the dust of the earth abides in the love of the One who formed it, may I abide in Christ this day.

Orange Juice

And he is the head of the body, the church; he is the beginning and the firstborn from among the dead, so that in everything he might have the supremacy.

COLOSSIANS 1:18 NIV

BACK BY POPULAR DEMAND

The Big Breakfast

Not only is Jesus the firstborn, he is the twice-born. The role that the Father gave to the Son at the very founding moment of the universe, he gives to him again in the new, redeemed creation. Jesus has not insisted on his rights as the firstborn over creation; he has entered the tomb and become, for us, the firstborn from the dead.

The triumphal procession of the creation, in which Jesus strides out at the head of all that has been made, rejoicing in the colour and beauty of the universe, is replayed as the triumphal procession of redemption. This time around, Jesus heads up the parade of those brought back from sin and death, those liberated from the curse of Eden.

There can be no room left, Paul insists, to question the supremacy of Christ. In creation, the Father gave him top billing – in redemption he has earned it all over again. The triumph of Christ is total. Satan may as well cower in the corner – there is no place for him in this parade.

Continental

Just as the creation reflects the character of Jesus, so will his new 'project', the Church. It is the same awesome, creative power that is at work. All the love that God poured into the making of the universe, he pours now into fashioning the Church.

Coffee

Praise to you, Lord Christ, for you have defeated every power that has set itself against you. Praise to you, Lord Christ, for you have won the final victory. Praise to you, Lord Christ, firstborn from among the dead.

Orange Juice
For God was pleased to have all his fulness dwell in him …

COLOSSIANS 1:19 NIV

GOD-IN-YOUR-POCKET

The Big Breakfast
With seamless logic, Paul moves from the glorification of Christ to his incarnation. This same Christ, Creator and Sustainer of the universe, became human.

He entered the flesh of Mary, became a single cell that split into two and then four. He grew to be a Polly-Pocket-sized embryo, then a baby, then a child, and then a full-grown adult. And at every stage of this journey, from the single cell invisible to the human eye to the man who laughed and cried with his disciples, God was pleased that his fullness should be in Christ.

Paul hardly pauses for breath at this point – as if he wasn't describing the deepest mystery of the universe. But he is. This is a puzzle that even Mulder and Scully couldn't fathom, a mystery beyond the greatest of minds – that it is possible for the God who made the universe, and who is by definition beyond it, to invest the fullness of his being in a single human cell.

This is God's ultimate affirmation of created matter: the ultimate expression of an unimaginable love. A faith founded on anything less is not the Christian faith.

Continental
The world may have its wonders, ancient and modern, but the universe holds no wonder more worthy of awe than the wonder of God-become-man.

Coffee
There is no structure in the universe big enough to contain God, and yet there is no structure so small that he cannot enter into it.

Orange Juice

… and through him to reconcile to himself all things, whether things on earth or things in heaven, by making peace through his blood, shed on the cross.

COLOSSIANS 1:20 NIV

HOLD EVERYTHING!

The Big Breakfast

There is a clear symmetry, for Paul, between creation and redemption – a symmetry centred on Christ. Just as all things are made by and for Christ, so all things achieve their redemption in him.

These are important concepts for the followers of Jesus. We experience the love of Christ in the micro-scale of our own lives. It is because of what Jesus has done *for me* that I choose to follow him.

But Paul wants us to understand that the victory of Christ is more than this. There is no word bigger than 'all' – nothing is beyond the scope of Christ's victory. The Christ of Calvary is the Christ of cosmic salvation – the 'all things' of creation becomes the 'all things' of redemption. The work of Christ is the biggest rock ever thrown into the pool of history, and the ripples go on spreading – reaching to the very edges of the universe.

Jesus did not die to save your soul. He died to rescue all things from the curse of sin and death.

Continental

How long would it take to write a list of 'all things'? Time itself would not be long enough. This is the measure of the victory that Christ has won.

Coffee

Take a moment to look around you, right where you are. Make a mental note of the things you see, and consider this: *all* these things are accounted for in the redeeming work of Christ.

Orange Juice
You are the salt of the earth … You are the light of the world.

MATTHEW 5:13-14 NIV

HU:MANIFESTO

The Big Breakfast
Ever since studying the Sermon on the Mount at school at the age of 14, I have been haunted by a single question – *Who?* Who is Jesus speaking to when he says, '*You* are the salt of the earth and the light of the world'?

He can't be addressing the Jews, since, by his own admission, God's revelation is now spilling out beyond its Hebrew borders. But nor can he be addressing the Church, since it hasn't yet come into being – and any such address would make no sense at all to the ad hoc crowd gathered on the hillside.

The answer I have come to is that Jesus is addressing humanity. *As humans* we are called by God to be salt to the earth. *As humans* we are to bring light to the creation. This is Jesus' reiteration of the 'Cultural Mandate' of Genesis – the call to women and men to take up their God-given role as preservers and developers of the creation. The Sermon on the Mount is Jesus' statement of the role of humanity in the cosmos. The call to follow Christ is the call to be human.

Continental
By pigeonholing Jesus as a teacher of religion, have we stripped him of his power as a teacher of life?

Coffee
The holy and life-giving God, teach you to reverence all his works, to praise him in all you do, to share in his work of creation, and to live to his glory.
(David Adam)

Orange Juice

But if the salt loses its saltiness, how can it be made salty again?

MATTHEW 5:13 NIV

PASS THE SALT

The Big Breakfast

To the Jew, salt was rock-salt — essentially a mixture of sodium chloride and rock dust. Pure salt as we know it was unavailable, and the purity and quality of the mixture varied — hence the possibility of 'salt' without 'saltiness'.

The rocky dust in your hand might look like salt, but it is powerless — in the Greek, 'dull' or 'moronic'. It has no edge or taste. It will neither preserve the freshness of food nor enhance its flavour.

Such is the fate of humankind without the wisdom of God. We may look like the bosses of creation, but we will lack the insight, the creativity, the dynamism to bring the best out of all that God has made. We will neither preserve the goodness of the earth, nor add flavour to its fruits. The cosmos will go on without the vital spark that God intended us to bring.

What can bring that spark back? Jesus doesn't answer the question, but leaves it hanging. This is the need he has come to meet. This is the mission of Christ.

Continental

What gifts and insights has God given you for the benefit of his cosmos? When it comes to using them, are you salty, or dull?

Coffee

'Your God is too small,' J. B. Phillips once wrote. Ask God to give you a glimpse of the sheer breadth of his purposes for the creation.

Orange Juice
You are the light of the world. A city on a hill cannot be hidden.

MATTHEW 5:14 NIV

GIVE US A LIGHT!

The Big Breakfast
The image is of a city at night. From a thousand lamps and torches, light collects to blaze out across the valley. Jesus does not say that a city *should* not be hidden but that it *cannot*. The message to humanity is clear – for good or ill, what you do will be visible in the world.

God has given to the human race the capacity to make a difference in the cosmos – in intelligence and gifting, in talent and skill. Whatever we do with that capacity, it will make a difference, and the difference will be seen. Like the Great Wall of China, which, they say, is clearly visible from space, we make our mark on the world. And what a mark we have made – in ozone depletion; in mass starvation; in the destruction of thousands of species per day and deforestation at one acre per second.

We understand in individual lives that what is sown is later reaped – but the city on a hill is a picture of the corporate dimension. In the same way, Jesus is saying, 'Your sins will not be hidden.' The impact of humanity, for good or ill, will blaze out across the universe.

Continental
If you were asked to summarize the human record as stewards of creation, what words would you use?

Coffee
If you want to understand the Creator, seek to understand created things.
(Columbanus)

Orange Juice
Neither do people light a lamp and put it under a bowl.

MATTHEW 5:15 NIV

LIGHTING FIRES

The Big Breakfast
Until the harnessing of electrical power, there was no light without fire and no fire without light. In the time of Christ, to speak of light was to speak of fire.

Oil lamps – a clay reservoir of oil with a wick to give a single, fragile flame – were the main source of light in every household. Olive groves were significant in part because they provided the oil used for light: they were the power stations of their day.

The instinct to put the light under a bucket is not as senseless as it might appear. A single draught or gust of wind could snuff out the flame in an instant. Under a bowl, it could be protected from such a fate – but its light would be wasted.

The choice is stark. To be valuable, the light must be vulnerable – over-protect it, and it loses its purpose. Take the risk, Jesus is saying. Use your gifts; expose your light to the potentially harsh winds of criticism, rejection and failure. Without risk, there is no light.

Continental
Olive-oil lamps give out, with their light, fragrance and a measure of warmth. To hide your light is to deprive human culture of the fragrance of God, and of the measure of warmth that you might bring.

Coffee
Lord, grant me … that my lamp may feel thy kindling touch and know no quenching; may burn for me and for others may give light.
(Columbanus)

Orange Juice

Do not think that I have come to abolish the Law or the Prophets; I have not come to abolish them but to fulfil them.

MATTHEW 5:17 NIV

I FOUGHT THE LAW ...

The Big Breakfast

The annual Darwin Awards are given to those who promote evolution by removing themselves from the global gene pool in the least intelligent and most spectacular fashion.

1999's recipients included a terrorist who sent a letter bomb to an enemy, helpfully including a return address. When the postal service were unable to deliver the package, they returned it to him. He promptly forgot what it was, opened it and was instantly killed.

These words of Jesus are a letter bomb addressed to the Jewish leaders. On the surface, it seems innocuous to talk of fulfilling rather than abolishing the Law, but inside this package is the explosive truth that the Law alone is not enough. The Law stands in need of fulfilment because it is incomplete. It is not the full revelation of the nature and character of God.

The Old Testament scriptures were the sacred, untouchable, unchangeable core of the Hebrew faith. Jesus, with the audacity of a man who is either morally twisted, terminally insane or telling the truth, calls time on the partial revelation and drops the bombshell: the full picture of God is now here.

Continental

It is often hard, when we have boxed and labelled God in systems that we control and understand, to recognize and welcome fresh revelation.

Coffee

What are the structures that Jesus the revolutionary might demolish in your life? Make an honest inventory – and invite him to bring fulfilment.

Orange Juice

But God has blessed you, because your eyes can see and your ears can hear! Many prophets and good people were eager to see what you see and to hear what you hear. But I tell you that they did not see or hear.

MATTHEW 13:16–17

WHAT DO YOU SEE?

The Big Breakfast

Now that we know that Jesus was and is the Son of God, we tend to forget what else he was.

To his disciples, in the scintillating three years between the encounter that took them away from their nets and tax-tables and the resurrection that finally showed him to be God, he was above all else a *prophet*. Like Elijah before him, he took a small band of followers, travelled with them and showed them how to *see the world* differently.

The task of the prophet, the biblical scholar Walter Brueggemann writes, is 'to nurture, nourish and evoke a consciousness and perception alternative to the consciousness and perception of the dominant culture.' This Jesus did through parables and teaching, through miracles and acts of love.

In just three years, he established a vision of life so powerful that it has funded the imagination of the Church for 20 centuries.

Continental

How often do we simply accept things 'the way they are', without looking for alternatives? Might God be calling us to see with different eyes?

Coffee

Ask God today if there are areas in which you are seeing things the way they are – but he wants you to see them as they *can be*. Pray for the renewal of your *prophetic imagination*.

Orange Juice
So Paul stood up in front of the council and said: 'People of Athens, I see that you are very religious …'

ACTS 17:22

A MARS A DAY

The Big Breakfast
Paul's visit to Mars Hill has become something of a rallying-point for Christian cultural engagement. We know by this stage that Paul is the great Apostle and church-planter. He has demonstrated the keenest religious mind of his generation. But here he goes further – grasping philosophies less akin to his own experience; quoting poets known to the Greeks.

His arguments begin not with his experience but with theirs. Before speaking, he has taken time to walk the city. He has observed and absorbed the lifestyles of these intellectual seekers. Inwardly, he has registered disgust at the idolatry of the city, but outwardly, this is the very point at which he establishes rapport.

Paul's approach is clear – far from emphasizing how different Christians are from their pagan neighbours, he builds a platform of common experience. 'We all ask the same questions,' he is in effect saying. 'Now here are the answers I have found.'

Without common ground there can be no contact, and without contact there can be no conversation.

Continental
For Paul, evangelism is as much about making connections as it is about making converts.

Coffee
Creator God, you are the one in whom we live and move and have our being. Many are those who worship you without knowing your name. Make connections, we pray, that you might be worshipped, by name, throughout the earth.

Orange Juice

This God made the world and everything in it. He is Lord of heaven and earth, and he doesn't live in temples built by human hands.

ACTS 17:24

GODS 'R' US

The Big Breakfast

Having launched his journey on common ground, Paul is soon in uncharted waters. He introduces the Athenians to something more than an extra god to add to their 'Gods 'R' Us' worshipfest.

This God, he tells them, is not a statue with a name and a convenient address on Temple Street. You can't put him in a building, and you can't put him on a plinth. He is no less than the Maker of all things, the Creator and Sustainer of the cosmos.

With great subtlety, Paul proposes a total paradigm shift: from the polytheism that puts a god on every street corner, to the monotheism that worships the one God and Parent of us all. The Athenians had gods of their own, but they were not averse to adding new ones. Like a child swapping football cards, Paul suggests that all the little gods they can muster can't match the value of the one God he has found.

By the end of the conversation, 'a few men' have agreed to make the swap – and the conversion of an entire civilization has begun.

Continental

God meets women and men where they are – but he takes them where they have never been.

Coffee

Creator God, teach me to free you from the buildings and boxes I have made for you and to worship you as the God who is above all gods.

Orange Juice
He gives life, breath and everything else to all people.

ACTS 17:25

INTIMATE STRANGERS

The Big Breakfast
In his sermon in Acts 17 and in his letters, one of Paul's favourite words is 'all'. Christ is Lord over 'all things', and is the maker and lover of 'all people'.

In one sentence, Paul has established that every one of his listeners – and every person in Athens – is already indebted to this God. You don't have to know God's name to be loved by him. Paul may be a stranger in town, but this God of whom he speaks is not. He is here already, loving the people of Athens and giving them the very air they breathe.

Paul is speaking of a faith of which these people know nothing. The name of Jesus has never been spoken in the streets of this city. And yet, he affirms, there are no strangers in God's economy. There is no more intimate act than the sharing of breath. The Athenians may not yet know what it is to be close to God – but God, all along, has been as close to them as breathing.

Continental
There is no 'unreached people group' on earth amongst whom God is not already at work. There is no place on earth in which it is possible to say, 'God is not here.'

Coffee
Father God, though I can count the days and years in which I have known you, thank you that there has never been a day – not even a second – in which you have not known and loved me.

Orange Juice

From one person God made all nations who live on earth, and he decided when and where every nation would be.

ACTS 17:26

WE ARE A SKIN KALEIDOSCOPE

The Big Breakfast

Identity is a powerful force. Gangs will fight for it; races struggle for it; nations go to war for it.

There is something at the very heart of the human experience that looks for a sense of belonging, of *home*.

The God of whom Paul speaks in Athens does not love humanity in some generic, blurred sense – he sees the detail. God is aware of your nationality. He knows your culture and speaks your language. In bald terms, 'He knows where you live.' And he loves diversity. His kingdom is a kaleidoscope, a glorious salad-bowl with ingredients from every tribe and tongue tossed together.

Paul has challenged the Athenians to surrender their local gods and to worship the God of the universe. But the miracle of the incarnation is that a universal God becomes a local God. God wants you to know him as the keeper of the cosmos – the Lord of all – but he also wants to move into your neighbourhood.

Continental

'Think globally, act locally' is a slogan coined by the Green lobby and used by many organizations. It is also, according to Paul, God's strategy.

Coffee

Those who have ears. Those who have cares. Those who have fears. Those who have tears. Let them hear … and see … and feel … and breathe.
(From Mike Riddell, *alt.spirit@metro.m3*, Lion, Oxford, 2000)

Orange Juice

God has done all this, so that we will look for him and reach out and find him. He isn't far from any of us.

ACTS 17:27

MULLING IT OVER

The Big Breakfast

If you have the good fortune to walk the streets of Vienna in December, or ski in the mountains of central Europe, you will become familiar with one of the planet's greatest pleasures: mulled wine.

This warming, invigorating drink is made when herbs and spices are added to ordinary wine – and left on a slow heat until the flavours have thoroughly transformed the drink. The secret of mulled wine is the miracle of infusion – time bonds the added herbs so deeply into the host drink that separation becomes impossible. Similarly, have you ever stirred too much sugar into tea by mistake, and wondered why you can't stir it out again?

Thus, too, does the presence of God infuse the earth. He is not far from each of us because he bonds himself to the very atoms of the world in which we walk. Where does the natural world end and the supernatural begin? The veil between the two is wafer-thin. Whether we know it or not, our lives are steeped in God. Heaven and earth are close enough to touch.

Continental

The shortest measurable distance in the universe is the distance you must travel to reach God.

Coffee

Father of all, there is no place on earth from which I cannot reach you without even needing to stretch. Help me, today, to discern and acknowledge your presence everywhere.

Orange Juice

I am the gate for the sheep … I am the good shepherd. I know my sheep, and they know me…

JOHN 10:7, 14

SHEEPLESS IN SEATTLE

The Big Breakfast

There are two problems in relating these words to the 21st Century. The first is that few of us are shepherds. The second is that none of us are sheep.

Talk of shepherding invokes images of a rarefied rural peace that we experience only on occasional days off. Our lives are shaped more by Bill Gates than by sheep-gates.

We totally miss the life-and-death drama of this image. Safe pastures, for sheep, represent the sustenance without which they will die. To be led to pasture is not only to eat, it is to eat under the watchful eye of the shepherd: sustenance, safety and security rolled into one.

The sheep get to know the shepherd's voice because it represents their best hope of survival. Their fullness of life is built on this relationship of trust. The shepherd leads me well because he leads me to life.

Continental

The shepherd leads the sheep to food and safety. In what ways has the leading of God fed and sustained you, and brought you into places of security and safety?

Coffee

The Lord is my Shepherd, I shall not whinge.

Orange Juice
May God be gracious to us and bless us and make his face shine upon us ...

PSALM 67:1 NIV

US AND THEM

The Big Breakfast
Sometimes the smallest words we know are the most dangerous. The word us is a good example.

We are driven to form an 'us' around ourselves – to love and be loved, to belong. My most valued relationships are those that take me from being 'me' to being 'us'. 'Us' is one of the warmest words we use, and without it we are lost and alone.

But the danger is that our 'us' produces a 'them'. For every friend, there is an enemy – real or imagined. For every insider there is an outsider. The prayer, 'May God bless us ...' is silently echoed with the response, 'but not them'. When this happens, the word 'us' becomes one of the coldest in our lexicon. Ask a black South African how it felt to hear the 'God Bless Us' of the white regime during the years of apartheid.

The challenge is to learn that the 'us' we pray for can be *all of us*. Wherever we put a boundary marker, God's love flows beyond it – he longs to bless us *and* them.

Continental
If the 'us' of our prayers is not 'all of us', then it shouldn't be any of us at all.

Coffee
Forgive us, Father, that the *us* of our lives has been exclusive. Forgive us that we have sought your blessings on us alone. Bring us, we pray, to an *us* that truly is *all of us*.

Orange Juice
... that your ways may be known on earth, your salvation among all nations.

PSALM 67:2 NIV

WORLDWIDE WORSHIP

The Big Breakfast
As island-dwellers, the British are perennially conscious of their coastal weather system. On one particular day in the 1930s, the whole of the south coast was hidden in a deep and impenetrable fog. The response of a certain British newspaper was to run the headline: 'Fog in Channel – Continent Cut Off'. It never occurred to the writer that it is the island, not the mainland, that gets cut off on such days.

At the heart of worship, there is a world-embracing dynamic. God's desire is to be worshipped in all the earth – in every people group. Our problem is that our worship is so often fog-bound. Our prayers end where our national boundaries stand. We know that in theory God seeks worshippers from every tribe and tongue – but our own needs loom larger in our minds.

It is hard work to keep alive the global vision of God's purposes – but it is work to which we must commit ourselves. God longs for our worship to be deeper – but he also wants to make it wider!

Continental
Wherever you live on earth, less of the planet is close to you than far from you. How might this reality be reflected in worship and prayer?

Coffee
God of the global, widen my vision of your love. Lord of the local, deepen my awareness of your work.

Orange Juice
May the peoples praise you, O God; may all the peoples praise you.

PSALM 67:3 NIV

A NO-EXPORT COMMODITY

The Big Breakfast
When I worked for a time in a high-tech marketing organization, we wanted to import to the UK a new piece of technology developed in America. We were prevented from doing so because the inventor in question could not get an Export Licence from the US Administration. There were a number of reasons for this, but no room for appeal. If we wanted the technology, somebody here in the UK would just have to develop it.

A similar process is at work in mission. God longs for worship to arise in every people group: what he does not long for is that the technology of worship should be exported from one nation to another. We look for all people to praise God, but he looks for all *peoples* – the distinction is important. It implies that God recognizes cultural groupings – cultural identity is not swallowed by worship. People groups bring colour and diversity to the worship of God.

Authentic worship arises from within a people group – it cannot be imposed on it. You cannot export worship – only the truth that inspires it.

Continental
Worship by all peoples will be worship in all languages, cultures and styles. This is Technicolor worship – the monochrome version may suit *us*, but it cannot reflect the full measure of God.

Coffee
Open my eyes, Lord, to see the possibility of praise in all the cultures, languages and peoples of the world.

Orange Juice

May the nations be glad and sing for joy, for you rule the peoples justly and guide the nations of the earth.

PSALM 67:4 NIV

The Big Breakfast

There are some journeys that, no matter how short the distance, seem to take forever. The journey from the heart to the wallet is one. For many of us, the journey from worship to justice is another.

Worship is associated with God and us, with his work in our lives and with our feelings in response to his actions. The wider dimension of public justice belongs to some other arena – that of campaigning, social action and politics.

There is no such problem for the writer of this Psalm. The peoples of the earth will worship God because he is just. The ways of God are good news in a nation, bringing with them gladness and justice. People will be caused to worship God, the Psalmist contends, in response to the justice that he brings. Justice is as much a part of worship as singing.

Where the coming of 'Christians' to a nation brings with it not justice but oppression, the God in whose name they come is not worshipped!

Continental

We speak of a God who receives our worship, who hears our prayers and songs. God listens, also, for the voice of justice in the earth.

Coffee

As a song rises to the ears of God, as my prayer like incense comes to him, let justice also rise and the fires of mercy burn.

Orange Juice

May the peoples praise you, O God; may all the peoples praise you.

PSALM 67:5 NIV

WHERE SHEEP MAY SAFELY PRAISE

The Big Breakfast

Repetition is not always a bad thing. There are times when we need to hear the same words twice or more to get the message.

The Psalmist here is determined that we will know what it is that lies at the very heart of the Psalm: the desire that the peoples of the earth should worship God. Is this a cry for worship, or for mission – for contemplation or for action? It is a unified cry for both.

Worship without mission becomes selfish and finally destructive. Mission without worship has no goal or aim, and will be consumed by the immediacy of need. Mission motivated by worship acknowledges, as the Psalmist here implies, that praise is the mark of the presence of God. It is where God is known and at work that praise is heard.

To long for the praise of God to rise up in the nations is, in New Testament language, to long for the coming of his kingdom. Praise cannot be divorced from the action of God in the earth.

Continental

Where God is praised, something of the kingdom has come. The ultimate aim of mission activity is no less than to hear the worship of God rising up in every corner of the world.

Coffee

Lord God, where injustice has held sway, *may the peoples praise you.* Where oppression has kept the light of truth hidden, *may the peoples praise you.* Wherever your kingdom breaks out, in light and life and joy, *may all the peoples praise you.*

Orange Juice
Then the land will yield its harvest, and God, our God, will bless us.

PSALM 67:6

MAN BITES DOG!

The Big Breakfast
The oldest rule in journalism is this: 'Dog Bites Man' is not news; 'Man Bites Dog' is front-page news. This verse is one of the Old Testament's 'Man-Bites-Dog' headlines.

The expectation of the Hebrews, still very evident in our century, is that a good harvest leads to praise. When the crops come in, and our barns are full, we will give thanks to our God or gods. It is a deep human instinct to offer thanks for gifts received.

But this Psalm says something different – it says that praise leads to a good harvest! When we praise God, when we rejoice in the justice of his rule, *then* the land will yield its harvest. It is as if the very soil we work with is programmed to respond to the praise of its Creator.

This biblical principle is often misapplied by the salesmen of a comfort-fit prosperity gospel. But it remains true – praise works. Put first things first – offer your life as worship – and let God take care of the harvest. Where God is rightly worshipped, fruitfulness flows.

Continental
We may feel that we should invest heavily in our working lives, so that we can praise God in plenty – but God calls us first and foremost to invest in our worshipping lives, and leave the plenty in his hands.

Coffee
God my provider, whose praise is the substance of the very air I breathe, help me today to put first things first, and worship you before and above all else.

Orange Juice
God will bless us, and all the ends of the earth will fear him.

PSALM 67:7 NIV

THE FAME GAME

The Big Breakfast
Probably the most famous billboard advert in history was put out by the Democratic Party in the 1960 US Presidential election.

John F. Kennedy was running against Richard Nixon. The polling couldn't have been closer, and on the eve of the final, crucial vote, the Democrats knew they had to pull something out of the hat to tip the scales in their favour. The next day America awoke to billboards that held a huge photograph of Nixon and asked one simple question: 'Would you buy a used car from this man?'

As well as becoming a legend in communications studies, this campaign illustrates a universal truth: in politics and PR, appearance is everything. It is a truth with which the Hebrew mind would have been at home. There is a passion – a jealousy – in the Old Testament for the reputation of God.

The whole project of worship and obedience and the flowing of *Shalom* into our lives is geared to this outcome: that God should be famous to the ends of the earth.

Continental
Just how famous God becomes – how widely and deeply his fame spreads – may depend, in the end, on what kind of billboards our lives become.

Coffee
In the closest circles of my life, *Lord, may your fame spread*. In the furthest reaches of my world, *Lord, may your fame spread*. From the outset of my day to the ends of the earth, *Lord, may your name be known*.

Orange Juice
And he kissed all his brothers and wept over them.

GENESIS 45:15 NIV

YOU DON'T OWE ME!

The Big Breakfast
The possibility of total forgiveness is demonstrated in the life of the Amazing Technicolor Joseph. Tricked and deceived by his own brothers, he was robbed of his inheritance and sold as a slave.

Years later, the tables were turned. Joseph had gained wealth and prestige, and it was the brothers who stood before *him* to ask his help. It was within his power to have them thrown into jail. At the very least he could humiliate them publicly, and let them know how deeply he was wounded.

Joseph did none of these things, however – he wept before his brothers and embraced them. This was only possible because the debt they owed him no longer existed.

It is not enough to say, 'I forgive'; you have to back it up by wiping out the debt – so much so that when you are given the opportunity for revenge, you will pass it up. This is the measure of the forgiveness with which God has forgiven us – and it is the measure with which he urges us to forgive those indebted to us.

Continental
There are some for whom the debt to be forgiven has a crushing, years-spanning weight. God neither demands nor expects glib obedience. Forgiveness is a place we are journeying to – even if, for some, the journey is long.

Coffee
Help me, God of the second chance, to cancel the debts of those who owe me. Where this is a hard journey, help me to take the first small steps.

Orange Juice

My dear friends, we must love each other. Love comes from God, and when we love each other, it shows that we have been given new life.

1 JOHN 4:7

MY LOVE IS YOUR LOVE

The Big Breakfast

Everyone who loves touches God. Whoever gives love celebrates the presence of God in their life in the measure in which they give that love.

Love is the sign of God in the creation. If God were not present, set loose by the power of his Spirit to roam the roads of the cosmos, there would be no love. Every time a child is loved, God is worshipped. Every time, for the love of another, we overcome the love of self, God is worshipped.

The word 'love' is written through God like 'Blackpool' through a stick of rock – but in the same way, the name of God is written through love. Love is God's idea, God's project. God owns the intellectual property rights to the concept of love.

It is quite possible to put love to the wrong use, just as it is possible to experience corrupt and selfish forms of love. And it is quite possible to love in the name of other gods, or of no god. But the underlying reality, as sure as eggs come from chickens, is that love comes from God.

Continental

No one can contend that the hand of God has never been at work in their life unless they have never loved or been loved.

Coffee

If not for love, we could not know the name of God. If not for love, we could not seek him. If not for love, we would not feel the need for God. If not for love, we could not meet him.

Orange Juice
God is love, and anyone who doesn't love others has never known him.

1 JOHN 4:8

SENTIMENTAL SEDIMENT

The Big Breakfast
Each of us has our own strange habits and obsessions. One of mine is the need to clean stainless-steel sinks.

There is something that offends me in the fact that stainless steel is so quick to get stained – and there is nothing better to stain it with than tea and coffee leftovers. These regularly build up a presence in our sink, and from time to time I will go at it with bleach and scourer until it shines again. The sight of a gleaming sink satisfies me deeply!

There is a staining, though, that is not so negative – the stain of love. This is the sediment that builds up in our lives when we pursue the way of love. Just as tea poured down a sink will leave a residue, so love poured through our lives leaves its mark.

I have recently been challenged to explore the difference between being a Christian and being Christ-like. The former can be an institutional, historic commitment – the latter can only be a changed life. Christian or Christ-like – the acid test is love.

Continental
What is the test of Christian growth? How do you assess your own progress? The answer lies in a simple question: Do you love more?

Coffee
Father, even when I love at my best, I do not love enough. At my worst I barely love at all. Flood me, I pray, with the love that bears your name.

Orange Juice

God showed his love for us when he sent his only Son into the world to give us life. Real love isn't our love for God, but God's love for us.

1 JOHN 4:9-10

THE MIRROR CRACKED

The Big Breakfast

For all that we are witnesses to the love and power of Christ, we are not the final measure of God's love. We know that our love is partial, dimmed, obscure and corrupted by self-interest. We know that we will never love enough.

The work of love in our lives is like the slow erosion of rocks in the flow of waves or a river. It is like the growing and maturing of a forest; like the way a city, year by year, expands its boundaries. It takes time – and usually far more time than we expect. Love is a long-term investment plan – cash it in early, and the returns will be disappointing.

Our fear, as this time so slowly passes, is that the picture others see of Christ in us will not be enough. We wonder if our lives will let God down.

But here is the good news. God has taken the initiative to pour his life into Jesus for precisely this reason: so that perfect love is made visible. Jesus is the benchmark of love.

Continental

It is to Jesus, not to the Church, that we look to see the fullness of love displayed. He is the light. We are at best broken mirrors.

Coffee

Thank you, Father, that when my love fails, the love of Christ remains. Thank you that when little of you is visible in my life, everything of you is seen in Jesus.

Orange Juice
Dear friends, since God loved us this much, we must love each other.

1 JOHN 4:11

COSMETICS WITH A CONSCIENCE

The Big Breakfast
Anita Roddick took a simple idea – cosmetics with a conscience – and built from it a global commercial enterprise.

One of the great qualities of The Body Shop is that principle and values are so close to the surface. The primary principle – central from day one – is the refusal to sell cosmetics tested on animals.

Roddick was able to grow a chain of stores very fast because she was able to guarantee that this principle would be present in every shop and reflected in every product. The passion of the founder is transferred, with considerable success, to the end product. When Roddick appears on television supporting a particular campaign, those same concerns will be reflected in stores bearing The Body Shop name.

It is this same quality – which can be described both in terms of shared values and of brand loyalty – that the Apostle John is asking for. If God has so loved us, then surely we, of all people – we who come under his banner and retail his brand – should be marked by that same love.

Continental
If those who own the name of Christ do not live in the love of Christ, who will???

Coffee
As you have loved me, Lord, teach me to love. As you accept me, teach me to accept. You tolerate my failures – teach me tolerance, Lord.

Orange Juice

No-one has ever seen God; but if we love one another, God lives in us and his love is made complete in us.

1 JOHN 4:12

WHEN LOVE CAME TO TOWN

The Big Breakfast

Conception is one of the more enjoyable activities written into God's creation order. Through the passion and love of a couple, something new begins. Darkly, secretly at first, in a hidden place, a new life begins to grow.

In time the new form becomes visible. Later still, through birth, we welcome a new being to the human family. But even this is just a stage – the growing goes on. And when physical growth has ended, years later, and decline sets in, there are still senses in which the growing goes on to the very point of death, and beyond.

Life itself is a never-ending adventure, a journey to the deepest reaches of eternity. In the same way, love is a journey towards completeness. When we let God in, something begins in and amongst us. It's a growing thing. Love may at first take hold in secret places, but in time it will break the surface. And the growing will go on forever.

God has committed himself to this process – he will never stop loving us until his love is made complete in our being.

Continental

When we receive God, love comes to town. A new force and power becomes present in our lives and community.

Coffee

O Lord our God, when Christ comes, Love comes. You make everything new. Transform the poverty of my being to reflect the riches of your love.

Orange Juice

You people are like children sitting in the market and shouting to each other, 'We played the flute, but you would not dance! We sang a funeral song, but you would not mourn.'

MATTHEW 11:16–17

THE MOURNING AFTER

The Big Breakfast

The story is told of two sisters. One was a born optimist, of cheerful disposition and soaring vision. The other was a confirmed pessimist, whose vision, like her chin, rarely rose above floor level.

In an attempt to redress the balance of the two, their parents decided one Christmas to fill their stockings differently. To the pessimist, they gave a sackful of good things – dolls, toys, chocolates and clothes. In the stocking of the optimist they put only horse-manure.

On Christmas morning, the pessimist was as glum as ever, complaining about the choice of colours and styles and listing all the gifts she *hadn't* been given.

The optimist, meanwhile, was dancing through the house, alive with joy. Her parents couldn't understand why, until they got closer and heard her say, 'I just know there's a pony out there somewhere!'

Continental

To the glum all things are glum. What might it mean to make the positive decision to dance?

Coffee

Each day may I remember the sources of the mercies/Thou hast bestowed on me gently and generously;/Each day may I be fuller in love to Thyself.
(From *Carmina Gadelica*, III, quoted in Esther De Waal, *The Celtic Way of Prayer*, Hodder and Stoughton, 1996)

Orange Juice

Jesus called out with a loud voice, 'Father, into your hands I commit my spirit.' When he had said this, he breathed his last.

LUKE 23:46 NIV

FAMOUS LAST WORDS

The Big Breakfast

If the words of Jesus are important to us, then his *last* words must be especially so. How did he choose to use the breath that, even as he used it, was being squeezed from his body by the unbearable heaviness of dying?

He chose to commit himself to God. These are words of lifelong habit. Jesus did nothing in the moment of death that he had not done in every moment of life. At the Temple at the age of 12, in the wilderness when he was 30, with his disciples, with the crowds, alone in Gethsemane – at every landmark in the life of Christ there is abandonment to the love and will of the Father.

These are also words of hope. In Psalm 31:5, the same words are used by a writer who knows God as a rock and refuge, and looks with hope to be rescued from an enemy's trap. For Christ, no matter how great the pain or how frightening the prognosis, the central reality is that the Father can be trusted. This is a cry not of blind desperation but of intimate trust.

Continental

When you face pressure, what emerges – desperation or trust?

Coffee

Father, I abandon myself into your hands; I give myself, to you without reserve, and with boundless confidence, for you are my Father.

(Charles de Foucauld, daily 'Prayer of Abandonment', quoted in *Come Let Us Sing A Song Unknown*, Dimension Books, Inc., New Jersey,)

Orange Juice

O LORD, our Lord, how majestic is your name in all the earth! You have set your glory above the heavens.

PSALM 8:1 NIV

THE WONDER YEARS

The Big Breakfast

A story is told about the movie star John Wayne, who was not known for the depth of his intellect. When filming the biblical epic *The Purple Robe*, he played the centurion at the foot of the cross. The Director was not convinced by Wayne's rendition, in cowboy drawl, of the line, 'Surely this was the Son of God.'

'Say it with awe, John — say it with awe!' he cried through his megaphone.

Wayne acknowledged the instruction, and on the next take, drawl unchanged, said, 'Awe, surely this was the Son of God.'

Wayne is not alone in struggling to articulate awe in the contemporary context. In an age of machines and bureaucracy, in which prosperity, leisure and security are ensured through technological wizardry, words like 'majesty', 'wonder' and 'awe' come strangely to us.

But there is an awe, a majesty, invested in the earth, and it points us to God. The recovery of wonder is a project in which the Christian can profitably and legitimately invest energy and passion.

Continental

If the wonder of the created order is a sign of the majesty of God, it is ironic that those most inspired by the earth are often not believers at all.

Coffee

Father, the glory of the earth is *your* glory. The majesty of the skies is *your* majesty. The wonder of the stars is *your* wonder. I give you praise.

Orange Juice

From the lips of children and infants you have ordained praise because of your enemies, to silence the foe and the avenger.

PSALM 8:2 NIV

NO CONTEST!

The Big Breakfast

What comes out of the lips of children? Faltering words; giggles; spit; sick; chewed food; half-eaten lollipops that attach themselves to car seats with an adherence worthy of superglue.

God is not revealed in the twee, sentimental perfection that we imagine in children until we spend time with them. He is in the intricacy and intimacy of the world he has made – with all its mess and muddles. The danger of this Psalm is that we picture a soft-focus image of angelic sterility – and then impose that image on our worship.

But our God is a real-world God. We love our children when their faces are dirty; when they are hidden in unspeakable mess; when the smell that rises from them would be at home in a Devon farmyard. We bond with them because, in the midst of the mess, there is a miracle happening – new life, formed and growing; the sheer joy of innocent, unsullied love. The enemies of God are silenced by such joy. Against power and sophistication, the miracle of infancy wins every time.

Continental

This is praise: not a world delivered from ambiguity and pain, but a God who brings to us, in the midst of ambiguity, the miracle of life.

Coffee

The world was made to praise you, Father. Where I fail to do so, infants and rocks will shame me by their song.

Orange Juice
When I consider your heavens, the work of your fingers, the moon and the stars, which you have set in place …

PSALM 8:3 NIV

LET YOUR FINGERS DO THE WALKING

The Big Breakfast
There are many examples of fast finger-work. A weaver working a loom, where patterns merge and emerge with impossible speed and accuracy; Vanessa Mae or Nigel Kennedy making the most difficult violin playing look easy; Flea from the Red Hot Chilli Peppers playing the bass like a typewriter; your grandmother muttering as she knits, while across her knee a perfect sweater takes shape.

In each of these the picture is of a complex sequence of small movements carried out at great speed, but producing not a blur but the uplifting beauty of patterns in music and art. Finger-work speaks of intricacy and accuracy, of delicacy and detail.

To the Psalmist, the skies are like lace. There is craftsmanship and artistry in the paths of the stars. All too often we picture a big God, Thor-like, who booms across the universe and hammers worlds into being. Here we celebrate the delicacy of God. This is God the Weaver, God the Player and God the Holy Knitter. The Maker of the universe has a good eye and a steady hand for detail.

Continental
If the finger-work of God is this creative, then we, his creatures, are safe in his hands.

Coffee
God the Player, thank you for the music you have made. God the Weaver, thank you for the wonder of the world. God the Holy Knitter, thank you for the beauty you are bringing to my life.

Orange Juice

... what is man that you are mindful of him, the son of man that you care for him?

PSALM 8:4 NIV

LIVING IN SKIN

The Big Breakfast

In 1887 the artist Paul Gaugin painted what he thought would be his last work. Planning to end his own life, he intended the painting as a kind of visual suicide note.

Its title was etched onto the canvas itself, and captured the turbulence not only of Gaugin's life, but of the turn-of-the-century world in which he lived. It was called *Where do we come from? What are we? Where are we going?*

In bringing the three questions together, Gaugin was echoing the voice of the Psalms. In our own day, we often speak of the first and last of the three, but the middle question gets less attention. What are we?

The contradictions of the creation – its holding together of animal savagery and spiritual peace – are wrapped up in the very fabric of our human nature. It is our humanity that points us to God, but it is our humanity that makes it hard to reach him. The lowest depths and the greatest heights in the universe are alike found in the human heart.

Continental

There are many mysteries in the universe, but two of the greatest are these: What is it that makes us human, and why is it that God loves us so?

Coffee

What is humanity? *Father, teach us to know you.* That you are mindful of us? *Father, teach us to love you.*

Orange Juice

You made him a little lower than the heavenly beings and crowned him with glory and honour.

PSALM 8:5 NIV

MAYBE ANGELS

The Big Breakfast

Some childhood games surface in almost every culture. Hide-and-seek and tag are two of them. Another is a game played on the seashore, at the very boundary of ocean and beach.

The game consists of running forward as the waves recede, until you are almost in the ocean itself, then retreating up the beach as fast as possible when a new wave comes in. The objective can be simply expressed: to get as far into the ocean as you can without getting wet.

This is the unique possibility that God has carved out for women and men in the creation: to get as close to heaven as it is possible to get without actually leaving the earth. The phrase, 'a little lower than the heavenly beings' implies that once you get 'higher' than women and men, you leave the earthly sphere altogether. Whatever God has poured into his creation, he has given to women and men a special place at its head. There is no higher calling in the universe than the call to be human before God.

Continental

We are earth-bound – made for earth and deeply tied to its rhythms – yet in our hearts we sense the possibility of heaven.

Coffee

A child of the earth, I long for the freedoms of heaven. A child of heaven, I long to see the kingdom come to earth.

Orange Juice
You made him ruler over the works of your hands; you put everything under his feet …

PSALM 8:6 NIV

A STEWARD'S ENQUIRY

The Big Breakfast
The unique place of women and men in the creation is not only a statement of human identity. It is also a job description. We have work to do.

Throughout the biblical witness, there is an emphasis on this notion of caring on God's behalf for the world. The term most often used for this role is 'stewardship', which carries with it the idea of accountability. We have a task, and we will be taken to task.

With trembling hands, God holds out to us the totality of the world he has made and loves. Like Paddington Bear, we find a label on it saying, 'Please Look After This Planet'.

The property handed to us is not some vacant lot, some square of barren ground – it is the tumbling, sparkling, precious product of the artist's hand. Imagine an author asking you to look after a lifetime's worth of unpublished manuscripts – texts into which he had poured his life. God trusts us with his treasures because he loves and honours us; because we're family.

Continental
We know that we are called to trust God. We speak less frequently of the flip-side of the same coin. God, deeply and genuinely, trusts us.

Coffee
Thank you, Father, for the trust you have placed in me. Help me, day by day, to make good that trust.

Orange Juice

... all flocks and herds, and the beasts of the field, the birds of the air, and the fish of the sea, all that swim the paths of the seas.

PSALM 8:7-8 NIV

PLACE YOUR ORDER

The Big Breakfast

Underwater swimming is an exhilarating and stimulating experience. Whether you dabble in the shallows of a holiday beach, or plunge deeper where only an aqualung can take you, you sense the wonder of being in another world.

There are fish to see, and crabs; rocks and shells and plants. One thing that you won't see, oddly enough, is paths marked out for fish to follow. But the Psalmist who wrote these words is not, by that token, completely mad. What is being described here is the sense of order at the heart of the creation.

The diversity of species, the complexity of food chains and weather systems, the patterns and structures from rock strata to relationships – all of these reflect the beauty of God's design. Where once there was chaos, where the Spirit of a brooding God has hovered, there is now order. Not the sterile order of the factory or army, but the wild, organic order of a peacock's tail.

From molecules and microbes to the furthest-flung galaxy, the creation is an orchestra tuned to the praise of God.

Continental

Studies in chaos theory have helped us to see that there is beautiful coherence at the heart of creation.

Coffee

We stand before your beauty, Lord, as we stand before an ocean. Far beyond our vision or imagination, there is no end of you.

Orange Juice

O LORD, our Lord, how majestic is your name in all the earth!

PSALM 8:9 NIV

APR 07 2005

BOOKENDS

The Big Breakfast

There is something satisfying about a journey that ends where it began. The bookends that begin and end this poem of praise are these same words describing the majesty of God. The images that populate the verses in between are held by these words, like water held in two hands cupped together.

In that sense the Psalm is a picture of the whole created universe. Before anything was, there was the glory of God, and at the end of all things is that glory. Our world will end as it began – in the bosom of the majesty of God. The presence and love of a personal God is the frame within which creation exists – all of time and eternity are book-ended by his character.

Before all was, he is; after all is, he will be. He is the outset of every adventure and the goal of every quest. He is the opening chapter of every story, and the end toward which it moves. Starting-pistol and finishing-tape – God is our beginning and our end.

Continental

The two sentences 'In the beginning' and 'At the end' can both be completed with the same two words: 'God is.'

Coffee

Glory to the Father, and to the Son, and to the Holy Spirit: as it was in the beginning, is now and shall be forever, world without end. Amen.